SOLUTION TO STOP OVERTHINKING YOUR RELATIONSHIP

HOW TO OVERCOME INSECURITY AND NEGATIVE
THOUGHTS TO EXPERIENCE THE LOVING AND
FULFILLING LIFE YOU DESERVE

S.G.FONTES

CONTENTS

INTRODUCTION

"Love is an endless mystery, for it has nothing else to explain it."

— *RABINDRANATH TAGORE*

Love. Various philosophers, singers, and poets have tried to capture "love's essence" in their sonnets. From Taylor Swift's songs to Shakespeare's drama, every story with the theme of love tends to raise your expectations or crush your dreams.

After all, let's be real. Relationships are a bit like roller coasters - exhilarating highs, scary drops, and the occasional urge to scream. Add a spritz of overthinking into the mix, and you've got yourself a one-way ticket to Anxietyville.

If you are wondering how that happens, then - picture this. You are at a party, and you've sent a text to your partner. Five minutes go by. Then ten. Pretty soon, your brain is hosting a Shakespearean tragedy, and you're convinced that a misplaced emoji is now a sign of impending doom.

Sounds familiar? Don't worry; you're in the sanctuary of fellow adventurers.

You might wonder, as you sip your tea (or coffee, no judgments here), reading the words of these pages, what is this going to be about? Well, as someone who has sufficient experience in real-life complications of relationships, I am here to get those brain cells of yours to *calm down*.

Across ten insightful chapters, I will take you through a scenic route filled with valleys of mindfulness and the peaks of positive thinking. We will laugh, maybe cry (happy tears, we hope), and most certainly learn as we discover tools and techniques to put those overthinking thoughts in their place.

First, we will traverse through the bustling "Questioning Quarters" of your mind. Here, you will always find your brain in a frenzy, trying to crack codes as if you are on a National Treasure hunt. "Was my partner's smile a secret love language or a cryptic message in an ancient love language?" Thoughts in this part of your mind are in overdrive, akin to a squirrel on a caffeine high. All this follows while your heart is tapping its foot impatiently, asking for a time-out.

Then, we set foot upon the towering "Summit of Doom." Here, overthinking triumphantly hoists its banner. Picture your beloved not returning your call promptly. Rather than pondering the possibility of them being preoccupied, you find yourself scaling the slopes, occupied by thoughts like, "They've secretly run off to join a spy group to escape our relationship!" A narrative fit for a Hollywood thriller, indeed, but in reality, it leaves you isolated in your life and relationship.

Next, we will make our way to "Sleuth Street" – a tribute to Hercule Poirot himself. Here, every text message is a treasure trove, and every conversation is an ancient scroll. A simple "Ok" in a message? Oh, that's a puzzle wrapped in an enigma! With your detective hat and trusty magnifying glass, you might find yourself trying to decipher the meaning of something that is not even that deep! After all, sometimes, more often than not, an okay is simply an okay (okay? okay).

Following it, we'll sneak a peek into the "Drama Alley." The imagination here knows no bounds; it's a true spectacle! Brains here direct and star in grandiose epics, with "Doomsday Love" playing to a packed house. The sweeping ballads of "We're Doomed!" play on a loop. Here, every minor detail and every text message becomes a cue to doom; that may not be happening! See, it's enthralling, but I can bet your heart longs for a sunny, feel-good rom-com.

Our final port of call is the undulating waves of the "Ocean of Self-Questioning." Here, the relentless currents of overthinking buffet the shores of conviction. You might feel akin to a lone pebble amidst waves, interrogating your worth and affection. The undertow of negativity persistently beckons you, growing more formidable with each return. This ocean is boundless, but let it be known you are not rudderless; your anchor lies in your intrinsic value and love.

Now, let's be honest; Worryville is a delightful, albeit high-strung, place. Your vibrant emotions and mental gymnastics are a testament to your big, caring heart. But let's not let them dictate your life's script, okay? After all, there's more to life than relationships that make you feel strung out. Sometimes, more often than not, your blazing mind needs a cool iceberg to relax and melt again. Sometimes, all we really need is someone who will understand our emotions, our constant need for reassurance, and just be there.

No matter how sweet that sounds, although this is seldom achieved. In a world like ours, everyone is too busy saving themselves. But you are not alone, dear reader. Whether these are scars from old relationships that felt like battle-fields at every turn or these are nuances of experiences that you saw your friends go through. I am right here to guide you through.

In order to move forward in life and away from these shackles, you will need to bear in mind that these thoughts are mere vistas within the tapestry of your partnership. They are places to traverse but not to forge a home in.

In the upcoming pages, I shall be your faithful guide, ushering you through uncharted terrains where the breeze is liberating and the panoramas instill solace. We shall traverse the rich tapestry of your past experiences and ingrained patterns.

Through reflection and revelation, you shall discover the invaluable pearls of wisdom that reside within you. But the journey doesn't end there; we shall transform these pearls into a beacon of self-awareness, shedding light on the intricate dance of your relationships. This knowledge is a treasure beyond measure, paving the way for immeasurable personal growth and self-discovery. Together, we will take measured steps toward a more enlightened self.

Moreover, we'll cultivate the serene gardens of self-care, which yield the flowers of mutual love. As you master the delicate art of expressing your desires and establishing balanced boundaries, witness the unfolding of a deeper, more meaningful union with your partner.

By the end of this book, you will find yourself equipped with a newfound prowess, navigating effortlessly to the welcoming harbors of a fulfilling, joyous, and harmonious bond with your cherished companion in love.

With a heart alight, let us embark upon resplendent isles of self-love!

Oh, and don't worry, this isn't the Hogwarts Express - no magic wands or spells here. But, by the end of these pages, you'll feel a little bit like a wizard, wielding the magic of self-awareness and positivity to build the relationship castle of your dreams.

So, fasten your seat belts, or rather, loosen them up (we're all about being relaxed here), and let's chug away from Anxietyville and head toward Serenity Town. Your heart, and perhaps your texting app, will thank you.

1

UNDERSTANDING OVERTHINKING IN RELATIONSHIPS

I f you are prepared to unleash the charismatic relationship maestro within, then fasten your seatbelts, kindred navigators! Let me tell you about this sly ninja – Overthinking. He's like a magician's rabbit, popping up out of hats when you least expect it, and it may well be plotting to overthrow the kingdom of your sanity. I wouldn't say it's Darth Vader's long-lost cousin. Still, it does have a knack for conjuring galactic-sized, wibbly-wobbly theories that would leave even a Jedi puzzled.

Picture this: You're texting a friend and simultaneously analyzing every single word they say, like a detective trying to solve a murder case. "What did they really mean when they said 'talk later'? Are they bored of me now? Mad at me? Did I do something wrong?" And just like that, you're jumping to conclusions faster than a kangaroo on a trampoline. Receive an angry face emoji from your partner? Well, now you're convinced they're about to break up with you. You *need* a 24/7 hotline for reassurance that your loved ones will not ditch you.

Overthinking in a relationship is like a runaway train barreling down the tracks. It starts slowly, with a few doubts here and there, but before you know it, it's gained so much momentum that it's almost impossible to stop. Suddenly, every little thing becomes a sign that your partner is hiding something from you. Did they take a little longer to respond to your calls? They're probably ignoring you. Did they not take your call at all? *Gasp*! Do they even love you?

It is a never-ending game of deciphering secret codes that don't actually exist. Your mind becomes an expert at conjuring up worst-case scenarios, and each new thought is more devastating than the last. You start to question everything – and let's not even get started on the dreaded *read receipts*. Seeing that someone has read your message without responding can send you into a tailspin of thoughts. Did they hate what you said? Did you offend them? Should you send another message to follow up? It's a slippery slope, my friend.

It's common to experience a few bouts of anxiety in the early stages of a relationship. Still, if you find yourself constantly overthinking every little detail, it could pose a real threat to the health of your relationship. Overthinking is a common issue known to infiltrate romantic relationships. Still, its cunning ways can also seep into relationships with friends, family members, or other important people in your life. It's when you begin to ruminate.

Think of ruminating as a hamster wheel for your mind, a never-ending cycle of negativity and distress. When you ruminate, you can't help but dwell on the causes and consequences of your negative feelings. You're stuck in a cycle of despair, and this vicious cycle can be a breeding ground for depression and anxiety, further worsening the current conditions.

But where does this runaway train come from? What fuels its relentless pace?

COMMON CAUSES OF OVERTHINKING

Often, overthinking stems from deep-seated insecurity or fear. It's like a sneaky little gremlin that hides in the dark corners of our minds, ready to pounce when we least expect it. And just like a gremlin, it can be challenging to get rid of. And when it comes to relationships, trust is the foundation upon which everything is built. It's like the glue that holds all the pieces together.

Without it, you're left with a shaky, unstable structure just waiting to come crashing down.

If you constantly doubt your partner's words and actions, it can lead to a whole lot of unnecessary stress and anxiety (MasterClass, 2022). You might find yourself analyzing every little thing they say or do, trying to read between the lines and find hidden meanings.

But when you have trust in your relationship, you can relax and enjoy being with your partner. You can take their words at face value, knowing they have your best interests at heart. And that's a feeling you just can't put a price on.

The problem with overthinking is that it can quickly spiral out of control. You start to see patterns and signs confirming your negative thoughts, even if they're not there. Then, it becomes a self-fulfilling prophecy – you believe that the other person will hurt or abandon you, so you start to act in a way that pushes them away. The more you worry and obsess, the more likely you'll begin to see evidence of your fears. Maybe they are acting distant because they're going through a tough time at work, but in your mind, it becomes proof that they're just perhaps tired of you. It's a vicious cycle that can erode even the strongest relationships.

That's why it's so important to recognize when you're overthinking and take steps to break the cycle before it's too late. Remember that communication is key in any relationship, and it's better to ask your partner for clarification than to make assumptions based on your own fears and insecurities.

THE SIGNS AND IMPACT OF OVERTHINKING ON THE RELATIONSHIP

In this section, we will explore the tell-tale signs that you might be a certified member of the Overthinkers Anonymous Club (*Kidding!*)

1. **The Mind Flip-Flopper**: Your mind changes more often than a chameleon on a rainbow! Can't decide if you want Italian or Chinese for dinner? Yeah, that's you.
2. **Text Decoder Extraordinaire**: One "Okay" text from your sweetheart, and you can spin 10 different epic dramas. Is it just a response or an encoded cry for help?
3. **Text Composer Supreme**: Crafting a simple text for you is like penning a Shakespearean sonnet. Hamlet had fewer soliloquies!
4. **Human Voicemail**: If they've said it, you've stored it. Your partner's words are etched in your memory as if inscribed on stone tablets.
5. **Microscopic Magnifier**: That misplaced fork at dinner? It's not just cutlery to you - it's a full-blown cutlery crisis!

6. **Emotion Deflector**: Trusting your feelings is like asking a cat to do a salsa dance - it seems impossible!

7. **Self-Baffler**: You've spun so many theories that even your mind feels like it's stuck in a labyrinth.

8. **Perpetual Paranoia Patient**: Convinced your partner's miffed at you? Even when they're just pondering over pizza toppings.

9. **Gloom's Best Buddy**: Even when things are brighter than a sunny day, you see rain clouds brewing.

10. **Apology ATM**: "Sorry" isn't just a word for you; it's your go-to response for everything.

11. **Plan Maestro**: Spontaneity for you is as appealing as a horror movie to the faint-hearted!

12. **Reassurance Junkie**: A little affirmation? You crave it like a coffee addict on a Monday morning.

13. **Future Gazer**: Living in the moment for you is like trying to catch a greased pig at a county fair!

14. **Second Opinion Seeker:** Your friend's judgment is your sacred oracle. They know better, right?

15. **Gut Feeling Denier:** Trusting your gut? It's as foreign as speaking Klingon.

16. **Reluctant Relationship Ender:** Breaking up? Only when pigs fly!

Recognized some of these in yourself? Fear not, for awareness is the first step towards becoming the over-thinking-conquering warrior you are destined to be! But before we move to that part, it is important to look at the impact of all this on your relationship.

Let's dive into the tumultuous sea of overthinking and fish out some pearls of understanding about how it can churn up waves in your love boat.

a. **You don't enjoy the present**: Imagine your relationship is a scenic road trip. Overthinking is like being fixated on the GPS rather than looking out the window and enjoying the breathtaking views. Instead of basking in the sunshine of love and joy, you're in a raincoat, anticipating storms that might never come. The present becomes like a fleeting ghost – constantly there but never fully grasped.

b. **Your partner can feel misunderstood**: Your brain is staging an opera, with every casual comment by your partner morphing into an intense aria. You might interpret their words like they're speaking in riddles. When you react to the imaginary dragons your mind has conjured, your partner might feel like they've been teleported to an alternate reality. They're waving at the "I didn't mean it like that!" flag. Still, overthinking has your relationship translating English to Martian and back.

c. **You have a hard time connecting with your partner**: Overthinking can be like an overzealous but terribly misinformed tour guide between you and your partner. It guides your thoughts and reactions down winding paths that lead to Nowhereville. The connection gets as patchy as a phone signal in the woods. You might be physically together, but mentally, you're in different dimensions, trying to solve puzzles that don't exist on the other side.

d. **You always want to be in control**: With overthinking as your sidekick, you might fancy yourself as Captain Control of Relationship Land. You try to steer everything: emotions, events, conversations. It's like trying to tame a wild river with a teaspoon – it doesn't work. Love is about flow and spontaneity. When the grips of control are too tight, the relationship can't breathe (Unilacke, 2018). The magic of unexpected moments is suffocated under schedules and imagined scenarios.

So, how do we anchor our love boats in calm waters? The truth is relationships thrive on open and honest communication. Without it, you're left to fill in the blanks on your own, and that's where the overthinking begins. It's like a pesky mosquito that won't stop buzzing in your ear. You swat at it; you try to ignore it, but it keeps coming back. Before you know it, it's all you can think about. You begin to analyze every little detail, every word, every gesture. And guess what? The more you think, the more confused you become and the more you overthink.

It's vital to recognize when overthinking has grabbed the wheel. Learn to let the present be your North Star, communicate openly, and trust the gentle waves of connection. Be brave enough to release the reins sometimes, and watch as your relationship sets sail on a voyage more beautiful than you could ever plan or predict.

THE IMPORTANCE OF BREAKING FREE FROM OVERTHINKING FOR A FULFILLING BOND

Fear not, for there is hope! It may seem impossible to overcome Overthinking, but you can break free from the web with the right tools and mindset. Start by identifying your triggers and recognizing when your mind is spiraling out of control. Then, try reframing your thoughts and focusing on your relationship's positive aspects (Smith, 2019). Remember that communication is key; don't be afraid to talk to your partner about your concerns. With persistence and effort, you can emerge from the web stronger and more connected than ever before.

One way to distract yourself from overthinking is to immerse yourself in activities that require your full attention, like playing an instrument or trying out a new recipe. Not only will this keep your mind occupied, but you'll also be able to create something tangible to be proud of. It's a win-win!

If you're feeling particularly restless, try going for a walk or running outside. The fresh air and exercise can do wonders for clearing your head. Alternatively, you could lose yourself in a good book or watch a movie you want to see. Whatever activity you choose, make sure it's something that you genuinely enjoy and can fully immerse yourself in. Before you know it, your mind will be focused on the present, and the overthinking will be a thing of the past.

Or, you could get creative! Pick up a pen and start doodling, or grab a paintbrush and let your imagination run wild on an empty canvas (Smith, 2019). Allow yourself to get lost in the process and forget about everything else. Try your hand at baking that recipe you've had bookmarked for months. Whatever activity you choose, make sure it's something that brings you joy and helps you disconnect from overthinking (Smith, 2019). Trust me, the mosquito will eventually buzz away, leaving you feeling refreshed and recharged.

Another technique to combat overthinking is intentionally reminiscing past successes and victories. Reach out to your trusted friends and family members and ask them to help jog your memory. Remember that time when you aced that difficult exam? Or when you nailed that job interview and landed your dream job? Think of it as a mental highlight reel of your victories. Hold onto those moments and let them remind you that you are capable of greatness. Allow yourself to bask in the warmth of your past accomplishments and let them serve as a guiding light through the fog of overthinking. By doing so, you'll be able to shift your thinking down a different path, leading to a more positive and productive mindset.

A helpful tip is to make a step-by-step plan for tackling each problem. This not only helps to organize your thoughts but it also gives you a sense of control and direction. Break down the problem into manageable steps and focus on one step at a time. Not only will you feel more productive, but you'll also be less likely to get overwhelmed by the big picture. So, next time you find yourself spiraling into overthinking mode, take a deep breath, grab a pen and paper, and start taking control of those racing thoughts.

Here's a fun questionnaire I've designed to help you take control of that overthinking monster. These questions can help you determine what you're looking for in your next relationship.

So, please grab a cup of coffee, or tea, get comfy, and let's get to it. Also, remember to take your favorite pen and paper (or type it on your phone), and let's dive in!

1. Ready or Not?

Okay, first up, do you feel like you're truly ready for a new relationship? They say love is a battlefield, and they aren't kidding; it can be pretty intense! So, think about it. Are you in a good place emotionally and physically to invite someone new into your world?

2. Hoping for a Hopeless Romantic?

Do you know how you feel warm and fuzzy when you see a cute couple? Do you feel hopeful that someday you'll find your person? Or does the fear of repeating past mistakes stop you from feeling that way? Remember, each relationship is a new chapter.

3. Ex-Files: Closed or Still Open?

Are you still holding a torch for your ex? If yes, it's not the right time to jump into a new relationship. It's wrong to make someone your rebound. It's best to work on healing first before starting fresh.

4. Open Hearts Club?

Are you open to love, or are you setting conditions like, "I'd love to date, but I'm too old" or "I'd be in a relationship, but I'm broke"? If you're finding excuses, you may need more time to be fully ready. Love doesn't come with a rulebook, so staying open is best.

5. Pickiness: Quirk or Deal Breaker?

Do you find yourself nitpicking potential partners? It's okay to have standards, but if you're rejecting people for being unable to sing or cook, you might set the bar too high. Find someone whose quirks you can live with.

6. What Went Wrong Before?

If you have reservations about diving into a new relationship, it's time to look back. What went wrong in your previous relationship? What were the main issues? This isn't to place blame but to learn and grow.

7. And What Went Right?

On the flip side, what went well in your past relationships? Was there something your ex did that made you smile? Keep those positive things in mind as you navigate the dating scene.

8. Relationship Type: Casual or Committed?

What kind of relationship are you looking for now? A fling, a serious relationship, or something in between? Whatever it is, be sure to communicate that with your potential partner. It's a two-way street, after all.

9. Values: Aligned or Astray?

Do you share similar values with this person? It's not just about shared hobbies or favorite foods, but their core beliefs and how they react to situations. This helps you to see if you can build a solid connection.

10. Meeting Friends and Fam?

Could you proudly introduce this person to your friends and family? If you're hesitant, it might be a red flag.

Remember, the opinions of your loved ones can influence your decisions.

11. The Happiness Factor

Lastly, and most importantly, do you think dating again will make you happy? Are you ready to share your life with someone, or do you need some 'me time'? Remember, you can't pour from an empty cup. It would be best if you found happiness within yourself first.

So there you go, some food for thought. Take your time; there's no rush. And remember, the goal is your happiness, whatever form that may take.

Reflect on your answers like a sea captain plotting a course. Recognize when you need to dock at Self-Care Island for repairs before setting sail again.

Try practicing gratitude. Picture this: you're walking through a lush meadow, with the gentle breeze whispering sweet nothings, and you stumble upon a chest filled with golden memories, big and small joys, and the heartwarming bonds you share. This my dear, is the treasure of gratitude - a magical practice that can transform the ordinary into the extraordinary. We'll discuss more about it in chapter 8.

Why does Gratitude Valley deserve a pin on your life map? Well, the air here is infused with positivity! Breathing it in, you'll find that a thankful heart is like a magnet for miracles. It's the currency that enriches your soul without making your wallet a tad lighter. It connects you to the present moment like a live wire and helps you realize that life is pretty darn rich even without that lottery win!

Next, you might also be interested in giving mindfulness a try! The essence of mindfulness is the ancient art of being fully here and now, relishing each breath like a bite of your favorite dessert.

"Why mindfulness?" you might ask, with a raised eyebrow. Well, let me paint a picture for you. Imagine a world where the sirens of stress lose their voice, and the quicksand of overthinking can't suck you in. Every sense is as sharp as an eagle's eye, and your heart's as open as the vast sky. That's Mindfulness Land!

Now, let's take a moment to look ahead and see what's coming up. Are you ready? It's Chapter 7! In this chapter, we will delve into Mindfulness Techniques. We'll explore ways to enhance our mindfulness, such as focusing on our breath and utilizing helpful resources. These techniques will guide us to be more present and fully engaged in the present moment.

You can also challenge distorted thinking by being the detective of your own mind! Keep an eagle eye out for the sneaky gremlin of negative thoughts - question if it's feeding you an exaggerated or biased story.

Remember to examine your thoughts like a detective on a case. Gather evidence to either support or dispute what's going through your head. You can do so by trying to see the situation from a different perspective – maybe that of your coolest and most relaxed self.

Next, ask yourself if this issue will still matter in the future. Picture yourself down the line. Will this be a blip on the radar or a defining moment? Then, just like a good friend would, give yourself some comforting advice. You're the star of your own life. Time to take charge of your thoughts!

Also, on another note, have you considered finding a way to calm your mind? It's important because when your thoughts are buzzing around, finding a way to calm down can really help. It allows you to stay focused on the present moment instead of letting your worries lead you astray. Being present stops your worries from taking you on a whirlwind trip around the globe.

Grounding can be done in various ways, like focusing on your breath, feeling your feet on the ground, or even hugging your favorite plushie (Teddy bears need love, too!) (Therapist Aid, 2018). It's about using your senses to anchor yourself to the present.

Now, for the exciting part: At the end of this chapter, you'll find a treasure trove of Grounding Techniques worksheets specially crafted for you! Think of it as your map and compass in this grounding adventure.

Lastly, develop your self-esteem. Having self-esteem is like being a proud peacock showing off its colorful feathers. Overthinking? Not on self-esteem's watch!

So, how can you do that? First, you should learn how to cheer for little Victories. Throw a mini-party for small wins, like enjoying a hot coffee or nailing a task. Every little victory is like a shiny new feather.

Remember, sometimes, you have to be your own hype person. Chat with yourself like you're your best bud, full of kindness and a sprinkle of 'you got this.' Also, keep in mind that you need to choose friends who make you feel like a million bucks. If someone's a bummer, wave them goodbye.

Learning your self-worth and accepting that you're worthy of good things in life is step number 1 in building a healthy relationship with yourself and your partner. As for the next stop of our journey, we'll look at how to deal with jealousy and insecurity in a relationship. As common as it may be, these feelings can be dealt with in a healthier way, and I'll walk you through the process.

GROUNDING TECHNIQUE WORKSHEET: RELATIONSHIP ANCHOR

Overthinking can be like a tidal wave in relationships, pulling you into an ocean of stress. The Relationship Anchor is a creative grounding technique to help steady your ship. It uses a combination of visualization, self-reflection, and sensory awareness. Let's set sail!

Materials

- A quiet space
- A piece of paper
- Pen or pencil
- A small object that comforts you (e.g., a smooth stone, soft fabric)

Procedure

Step 1: Find Your Safe Harbor

Find a quiet space. Take a deep breath and imagine your mind as a ship sailing through calm waters. This is your safe harbor, a place where your thoughts are still and your emotions are at peace.

Step 2: Visualize Your Anchor

On a piece of paper, draw an anchor. This represents the grounding in your relationship. Label each part of the anchor with different aspects of your relationship that make you feel secure (e.g., love, trust, communication).

Step 3: Feel the Weight of the Anchor

Hold the small comforting object in your hand. Feel its weight. This is your anchor's weight, helping to ground you. Close your eyes and imagine lowering the anchor into the water, creating stability for your ship.

Step 4: Identify the Storm

Think about a recent situation where you overthought your relationship. Please write it down above the water-line next to your ship. This represents the storm your ship faced.

Step 5: Drop Anchor

Write down what made you overthink (e.g., jealousy, fear). Then, think about how the aspects of your anchor can help ground you. Write one positive affirmation next to each part of your anchor.

Step 6: Sensory Awareness

Close your eyes and take five deep breaths. Feel the object in your hand. Visualize your ship steadying as the anchor reaches the sea floor.

Step 7: Reflect

Open your eyes and look at the anchor on the paper. Reflect on how the positive aspects of your relationship can help you during times of overthinking. Make a mental note to remember your anchor next time the storm begins to brew.

Step 8: Keep the Anchor Close

Fold the paper and keep it somewhere accessible. Whenever you feel overthinking, take hold, take it out, and remember your anchor.

To Remember,

Use this worksheet whenever overthinking tries to steer your ship into rough waters. Your strong anchor will help you find your way back to the safe harbor of a loving and grounded relationship.

Grounding Technique

5-4-3-2-1 Technique

So, you've been through a tough time, and having those not-so-great symptoms like flashbacks and anxiety is normal. But don't worry; we have some cool grounding techniques to help you! These techniques work like magic by shifting your attention away from those pesky thoughts, memories, or worries and bringing you back to the here and now. Let's dive in and get grounded!

5-4-3-2-1 Technique! Let's do this! Get ready to embrace your senses and notice the awesome details around you.

•• What are 5 things you can see? Look for the nitty-gritty stuff like funky patterns on the ceiling, the way sunlight dances on a shiny surface, or that random object you've never noticed before.

What are 4 things you can feel? Pay attention to the sensations all over your body, like the comfy touch of your clothes, the warm sun kissing your skin, or the coziness of the chair you're parked on. Oh, and grab an object and give it a good examination. How heavy is it? How does it feel to the touch? Let your hands do the exploring!

What are 3 things you can hear? Tune in to those sounds that usually fade into the background, like the steady tick-tock of a clock, the distant hum of traffic, or the rustling leaves in the breeze. Don't let those sneaky noises slip away! ♫

What are 2 things you can smell? Take a whiff of the air and catch those elusive scents floating around. Maybe it's a fresh air freshener doing its thing or the sweet aroma of freshly mowed grass. And hey, look around for something that emits a delightful smell, like a blooming flower or an unlit candle. Inhale deeply!

What is 1 thing you can taste? This is when to bring out your gum, candy, or a tasty snack! Pop it into your mouth and savor the flavors like a pro. Focus your full attention on the taste sensation. Mmm, delicious!

That's it! You've just rocked the 5-4-3-2-1 technique! By paying attention to the small and often overlooked details, you're on your way to becoming a sensory superhero.

Categories

Get ready for a whirlwind of categories and a crazy brainstorming session! Pick at least three of the categories below and unleash your creativity. Set a timer for a few minutes for each category and let the ideas flow. Ready? Let's go wild and come up with as many awesome items as possible! It's going to be a blast!

- Movies
- Countries
- Books
- Cereals
- Sports
- Teams
- Colors
- Cars
- Fruits & Vegetables
- Animals
- Cities
- TV Shows
- Famous People

Here's a cool twist to spice up the fun! Let's play the alphabetical game. Choose a category and start naming items in alphabetical order. For instance, in the fruits &

vegetables category, we'd go like "apple, banana, carrot," and so on.

Body Awareness

It is time to get in tune with your body! This body awareness technique will bring you right here, right now, by honing in on those juicy sensations. Get ready to feel it all!

1. Take a deep breath through your nose, count to five, and let it out slowly through your puckered lips. Ahh, feel that release!
2. Plant both feet firmly on the ground. Give those toes a little wiggle, curl, and uncurl them a few times. Take a sec to soak up the sensations tingling in your feet.
3. Let's make some noise! Give the ground a good stomp, and feel the impact shooting from your feet to your legs. Embrace those earthy vibes.
4. Ready those fists! Clench 'em tight, and then let go, release that tension. Repeat this power move ten times. Feel the stress melt away.
5. Push those palms together, really press 'em hard! Hold that pose for 15 seconds and let the tension soak into your hands and arms. You got this!
6. It's time for some hand magic. Rub those palms together briskly, feel the warmth building up, and hear that satisfying sound. It's like a mini-firework show!

7. Reach for the sky, baby! Stretch those arms up high like you're reaching for clouds. Hold it for 5 seconds, then bring 'em down and let 'em chill by your sides.
8. Take another round of deep breaths, in through the nose, out through the mouth.

Feel that calmness spreading through your body like a soothing wave. Your body loves the attention. Take a moment to bask in the calm vibes.

Mental Exercises

These exercises are discreet and can be done anywhere, anytime. Get ready to give your brain a workout and find the ones that work best for you. Let's dive in and have a blast!

- • Let's play "I Spy" with your surroundings. Name all the objects you see around you. Can you spot something cool and unusual?
- • Time to show off your skills! Describe step-by-step how to do something you're good at. Whether it's shooting a basketball, cooking your favorite meal, or tying a knot, break it down like a pro!
- • Get ready for some mathematical magic! Count backward from 100 by 7. Challenge accepted!
- • Pick up an object nearby and give it some serious attention. Describe its color, texture, size,

weight, scent, and any other unique qualities you notice. Let's appreciate the little things!

- • Let's play with words! Spell your full name, and then try spelling the names of three other people but backward. It's like a verbal puzzle!
- • Time to give a shout-out to the fam! Name all your family members, their ages, and one of their favorite activities. Let's celebrate those unique connections!
- • Flip the script and read something backward, letter by letter. Practice this mind-bending exercise for a few minutes. It's a mental gymnastics routine!
- • Get artsy in your mind's eye! Visualize an object and "draw" it mentally, or use your finger to draw it in the air. Let your imagination run wild—draw your cozy home, a speedy vehicle, or a majestic animal!

Excellent job, mental master! These exercises will keep your mind on its toes and give you a well-deserved break. Keep experimenting and finding what works best for you. Let's keep those thoughts in check and have some mental exercise fun!

Ask yourself questions

Let's dive into some self-inquiry to ground ourselves and shake off that anxiety. We will bring ourselves back to the present moment with some questions and answers. Grab a journal, quality paper, or anything you fancy, and let's get started!

Where am I right now? Take a moment to look around and note your surroundings. Are you at home, at work, or somewhere else entirely? Embrace the space you're in.

What day and month is it? Check-in with the calendar. Is it a sunny summer day, a cozy winter evening, or a beautiful spring morning? Feel the rhythm of time.

What season is it? Take a deep breath and sense the season in the air. Is it the vibrant colors of autumn, the blossoming energy of spring, the warmth of summer, or the peacefulness of winter? Let nature guide you.

How old am I? Reflect on the journey of your life. Count the years and celebrate the wisdom and experiences you've gathered along the way. Age is just a number, but it tells a story.

Where do I live, and with whom? Connect with the place you call home. Whether it's a bustling city apartment, a cozy countryside cottage, or somewhere in between, feel the love and security of your sanctuary.

Take a moment to imagine yourself at this very point. Reflect on the line of human ancestors who came before you, paving the way for you to be here in the present moment. Feel their presence and honor the journey that brought you here.

You're doing fantastic, my friend! These questions and answers will anchor you in the present, reminding you of your place in the world. Keep exploring, grounding, and embracing the beauty of being right here.

Positive coping statement

Crafting a powerful coping statement to tackle those moments of anxiety or overwhelm head-on. This statement will be your guiding light when the going gets tough.

"I am [your name]. This, too, shall pass. Every storm in my life has an expiry date. I will face this moment with strength and resilience."

Repeat this statement, savoring each word, and truly absorb the message. Recognize that painful memories and challenging events are temporary. They will not define me forever.

You're a rockstar, my friend! With this coping statement in your arsenal, you have a powerful tool to combat anxiety and overwhelm. Remember, you're stronger than you think, and brighter days are ahead. Keep repeating your statement, embrace the temporary nature of life's hardships, and watch yourself conquer every challenge that comes your way. You've got this!

2

MANAGING JEALOUSY AND INSECURITY: A HOW-TO GUIDE

T rust is a cornerstone in relationships. Trusting your partner is crucial to build a long and healthy relationship. An important aspect of this notion is the ability to trust oneself. Having faith that you can handle whatever life throws at you works wonders in the grand scheme of things. Let me narrate a story to make your understanding of trust, jealousy, and insecurity a bit clearer.

Once upon a time, in a quaint little village, there was an elderly couple, Martha and Harold. They were known to everyone as the epitome of love and understanding. One fine day, a troubled young woman named Anna approached them, seeking guidance to mend her turbulent relationship, marred by jealousy and insecurity.

With a warm smile, Martha began recounting a story from her youth. She revealed how, decades ago, when she and Harold were just newlyweds, they faced many challenges. Harold had a close friend named Sarah, with whom he shared a deep bond. Martha's heart was initially clouded with jealousy and insecurity about their relationship. She constantly worried that she might lose Harold to Sarah.

As days turned into weeks, she became more and more consumed by these negative emotions. One fateful evening, Martha overheard Harold and Sarah discussing a surprise gift they had planned for her birthday. It was a revelation - the two had only ever been friends, and her insecurities were baseless.

Fast forward to the present, and the wisdom in Martha's eyes was palpable as she told Anna, "My dear, jealousy and insecurity are the natural accomplices of love, but if we allow them to take the reins, they can tear down the strongest of bonds."

In this chapter, my dear reader, I aim to be your Martha when you walk the thorny path littered with jealousy and insecurity. The first step to managing these emotions is identifying the root causes. Is your jealousy a result of past experiences or insecurities? Or is it based on something your partner has done? Analyzing these emotions objectively is crucial to overcome overthinking.

ROOT CAUSES OF INSECURITY

Following are some of the significant reasons you may feel jealous or insecure in a relationship (Polk, 2022). To solve a problem, we have to look at the root cause and devise a plan to solve that issue accordingly.

a. Low Self-Esteem

Imagine your self-esteem as a delicate plant. When it doesn't receive enough nourishment, it wilts. A person with low self-esteem might find it difficult to believe that they are worthy of love, and this insecurity can fuel jealousy (Polk, 2022). Remembering that every soul is unique and deserving of love is essential.

b. Insecure Attachment Styles

Our early life experiences often dictate the patterns of our relationships. Insecure attachment styles, like anxious or avoidant attachments, can be the seeds from which jealousy sprouts (Polk, 2022). Embracing these attachment styles as part of our journey and working on them can be incredibly empowering.

c. Lack of Trust

Trust is the foundation of any relationship. When trust is eroded or absent, jealousy often creeps in. It's essential to recognize that building trust is akin to building bridges - it takes time, effort, and collaboration.

d. Unresolved Mental Health Issues

Sometimes, the mind is like a stormy sea, and unresolved mental health issues can make the waves of jealousy grow taller. Understanding and addressing mental health concerns with kindness and professional help can be the lighthouse guiding us through the storm.

e. Past Relationships

Our hearts carry the echoes of past relationships. Sometimes, these echoes reverberate in the present, instigating jealousy. Treasuring wisdom from the past while allowing the heart to embrace the present is vital.

f. Doubts over Long-term Potential

When we're unsure if a relationship has a future, uncertainty can breed jealousy. Reflecting on your desire in a relationship and engaging in open dialogue with your partner can pave the path forward.

g. Anxiety over Mismatched Relationship Goals

Different aspirations and goals in a relationship can cause anxiety, which sometimes wears the mask of jealousy. It's like trying to sing a duet with different lyrics. Understanding and aligning each other's dreams is the songbook for harmony.

h. Trauma from the past

Past traumas are like shadows; they follow us silently. When trauma is the puppeteer, jealousy can be one of the marionettes it controls. Acknowledging and healing from past traumas with support is akin to stepping into the light.

i. Stressful Events

Life is often an unpredictable roller coaster, and stressful events can leave us vulnerable. During these times, jealousy might sneak in through the cracks. Nurturing ourselves and seeking support during stress is like creating a safety net for our emotions.

j. Dealing with Loss

When we deal with loss, our hearts may clutch onto what we have left. This can manifest as jealousy. Recognizing this as a natural response to loss and gently allowing ourselves to process our grief is essential.

k. Poor Communication Skills

When words fail us, emotions might take the wheel. Poor communication skills can cause misunderstandings, leading to jealousy. Learning to express ourselves effectively is like crafting a compass for navigating relationships.

Remember, dear reader, that jealousy is a human emotion, and acknowledging it with kindness is the first step to understanding (Sheppard, 2021). Be gentle with yourself, and others, for hearts are gardens that flourish with love.

OVERTHINKING AND INSECURITY

In the tapestry of the human psyche, overthinking and insecurity are two threads that often entwine. Imagine your mind as a vast, magical library with infinite books. Each book represents thoughts, experiences, and emotions. Now, picture a librarian whose task is to efficiently organize and manage these books. When overthinking takes the stage, the librarian starts frantically flipping through the pages, absorbing chapters that feed insecurity and forgetting that there's an entire library to explore.

Let's delve into how overthinking fosters insecurity:

1. Negative Feedback Loop: Overthinking often leads to a negative feedback loop where the mind endlessly replays distressing events or worries (Sheppard, 2021). This constant looping creates fertile ground for insecurity to thrive, as the mind gets stuck on perceived flaws and doubts.
2. Distorted Lens: Overthinking can act as a pair of distorted glasses, magnifying the negatives and minimizing the positives. Through this distorted lens, insecurities appear far more significant and insurmountable than they are.

3. Imagination Overdrive: When the gears of overthinking are engaged, the imagination shifts into overdrive. It creates numerous 'What if' scenarios, mainly with a pessimistic outlook. This tends to feed insecurities, as one imagines all the ways in which things can go wrong, questioning one's ability to handle them.

4. Social Comparison: Overthinking often leads to excessive social comparison. One may ruminate over how their life, achievements, or appearance stack up against others. This comparison, more often than not, feeds insecurity as it's easy to feel like you're falling short in a race that doesn't indeed exist.

5. Paralysis by Analysis: Constantly analyzing and dissecting every word, action, or choice through overthinking can lead to indecisiveness and inaction. This paralysis by analysis' can feed into insecurities about one's own judgment and decision-making abilities.

6. Filtering Out Reassurance: When lost in the maze of overthinking, the mind tends to filter out positive feedback and reassurance from others. This deprivation of positive reinforcement exacerbates insecurities as the scale tips towards self-doubt.

7. Erosion of Present Moment: Overthinking often robs us of the present moment, as the mind is either entangled in the Past or anxious about the

future. This erosion of presence can lead to insecurities regarding one's ability to connect with others and engage fully in life.

Here's a simple way to understand how overthinking and insecurity are linked. Imagine you're in a brand new relationship and text your partner but don't get a reply for a few hours. Suddenly, your brain goes into overdrive with thoughts like "Oh no, are they mad at me?", "Have they lost interest?" or "Did I say something bad?" This non-stop thinking can make you feel insecure because you begin to doubt how solid the relationship is and whether you're good enough. In this situation, overthinking makes you insecure because you're getting worried and thinking there's an issue when everything might be fine. You can avoid feeling so insecure in your relationships by figuring out how to spot when you're overthinking and finding ways to manage it.

Understanding the dance between overthinking and insecurity is the first step towards composing a more harmonious inner symphony. The key is to gently guide the librarian of your mind, encouraging them to peruse the pages with care and intention and to sometimes leave the books on the shelf to breathe in the wisdom of the library itself. Through mindfulness, self-compassion, and seeking professional help, one can foster a mental landscape where thoughts are clouds passing by rather than storms to be swept into.

WHY DO WE GET JEALOUS IN RELATIONSHIPS?

Think of your feelings like a small garden. Knowing what makes you upset is like having a map showing where the cool stuff is hidden in your garden. But watch out! Among the nice-smelling flowers, there's a lousy weed named Jealousy that loves to grow.

Knowing what makes you jealous is like wearing special glasses that let you see under the ground. This helps you find out why the lousy jealousy weed is growing. Say your partner goes out with friends, and you feel jealous. It might not be just about them going out, but because something from long ago makes you scared of being left alone.

To understand why individuals tend to get jealous, picture this: your relationship as a giant kaleidoscope. It's vibrant, ever-changing, and can capture your heart. But occasionally, a shade of green (and we're not talking about the pretty emerald variety) sneaks into this colorful ensemble – we call it jealousy.

Let's get into the nitty-gritty of jealousy. There's a multitude of reasons why jealousy is triggered in a relationship. The Ghosts of Relationships past might be crashing your love party. Previous experiences with betrayal or abandonment could be the unwelcome guests making you see green.

Then there's the insidious Comparison Gremlin. This critter loves to compare your life and your relationship to those of others. If your bestie's partner is showering them with roses while you're getting daisies, the gremlin whispers, "See? They love each other more."

Oh, and let's remember the Invisible Ink of Unclear Boundaries. Sometimes, you might still need to lay out the terms and conditions of your relationship. If your partner is unaware that texting their ex at midnight is not on your list of approved activities, jealousy could sneak in like a cat on a mission.

So, why is it crucial to know our triggers? Being aware of what revs up the jealousy engine is like having a personalized treasure map. It leads you to the troves of your emotions and helps you understand the "whys." It's like turning on the lights in a room that's been dark for ages.

By recognizing these triggers, you become the grandmaster of your emotions. You learn how to tame the green beast or, even better, use its energy for good. It's like knowing the secret combination to a safe; suddenly, you're in control.

Moreover, it helps build the Golden Bridge of Communication in your relationship. When pinpointing what's eating at you, it's easier to express it to your partner without the conversation turning into World War III.

Remember, understanding jealousy is not just about warding off the green-eyed monster. It's about cultivating a lush, jealousy-free garden for your relationship to bloom. Think roses without thorns, rainbows without rain, and love songs that speak of joy. That's the magic that awaits when you understand and tame your triggers.

Now, let's talk about when jealousy crosses the line and becomes abusive.

Imagine a couple, Laura and Mark. They have been together for a year. At first, Mark's jealousy appeared harmless, even flattering to Laura. But as time passed, Mark's jealousy started taking a darker turn.

He began to demand that Laura cut ties with her male friends. He started insisting on having access to her phone and social media. The final straw was when he aggressively confronted a co-worker of Laura's at a company event, accusing him of trying to steal her away.

In this example, Mark's jealousy has crossed into the realm of abusive behavior. It is important to recognize when jealousy stops being just an emotion and becomes a tool for control and manipulation. This kind of jealousy is not rooted in love but in possession and fear.

Anyone who has experienced this knows that jealousy as a form of abuse is never justified. It's crucial to establish boundaries and seek help if necessary. Relationships should be sanctuaries of love, respect, and mutual growth, not cages wrought by the bars of jealousy.

WAYS TO COPE WITH JEALOUSY AND INSECURITY

Embarking on the journey to tame the stormy waves of jealousy and insecurity is both brave and nurturing. It is a testament to your dedication to cultivating a garden of love that is both vibrant and serene. Let's take tender steps together:

1. **Confront Your Fears:** Like gentle whispers in the night, listen to what your fears are telling you. Hold their hands and ask, "Why are you here?" Understanding the fears that fuel jealousy and insecurity is like turning on a soft lamp in a dark room.

2. **Address Your Expectations:** Reflect on your expectations for yourself and your partner. Are they entwined with love, or are they chains weighing down the wings of your relationship? Fine-tuning expectations to resonate with empathy and understanding is akin to tuning a musical instrument for a harmonious melody.

3. **Be Open and Honest:** Communicate your emotions to your partner with a heart as gentle as the morning dew. Let the words flow like a

stream, carrying the leaves of jealousy and insecurity, to be seen and understood by both.

4. **Accept That Jealousy is Hurting Your Relationship:** Acknowledge, my dear one, that jealousy can be like a thorn amidst the roses. Realize that it may pierce the tender bond you share with your beloved. This recognition is the first step towards removing the thorn with care.

5. **Admitting That You're Jealous:** There is a profound strength in vulnerability. Admitting that you're feeling jealous is like standing in the rain, allowing it to wash over you, and saying, "I am not afraid."

6. **Agreeing Not to Spy on Your Partner:** Trust, dear heart, is a sacred tapestry woven with threads of faith. Agree to not let the scissors of spying sever this tapestry. Hold your partner's hand and commit to trust as your guiding star.

7. **Discussing the Roots of Your Jealous Feelings:** Venture together into the depths of your jealousy. This shared journey through the caverns of emotions is a quest for treasures of understanding and healing.

8. **Making a Decision to Change Your Behavior:** With resolve as steadfast as the ancient oak, make the decision to reshape the paths you tread in love. Let the footsteps be gentle, mindful, and guided by compassion.

9. **Realizing You Cannot Control Someone Else, But You Can Control Your Reaction:** Understand that trying to command the winds is futile, but you can set the sails. You have the quill with which to pen your responses with grace.

10. **Seeking Professional Help as a Couple if Necessary:** Sometimes, the path may be rocky, and having a guide can be a blessing. Don't hesitate to seek out professional advice.

11. **Setting Fair Ground Rules You Can Both Agree To:** Together, craft the pillars supporting your bridge of love. Ensure these pillars are built with fairness, respect, and mutual agreement.

May your journey through the meadows of love be filled with the gentle breezes of trust, the sunshine of understanding, and the flowers of compassionate growth.

RELATIONSHIP SELF-ASSESSMENT: AN IN-DEPTH ANALYSIS OF STRENGTHS AND WEAKNESSES AND RECOMMENDATIONS FOR IMPROVEMENT IN YOUR RELATIONSHIP.

Analysis of response

You will rate each question on a scale of 1 to 5, where 1 is the lowest, and 5 is the highest level of satisfaction. Once you're done with all the questions, you can calculate the average score for each of the four main areas: friendship and intimacy, conflict management, shared meaning, and trust and commitment.

Friendship and Intimacy:

1. How often do you feel that emotional connection with your partner, like you're on the same wavelength?___
2. How often do you guys do stuff together that you both love and have a blast doing?___
3. How often do you feel like your partner really know you, like they understand where you're coming from?___
4. How satisfied are you with how much loving and physical intimacy you're getting in your relationship?___
5. How often do you show your partner how much you appreciate and adore them?___

Conflict Management:

1. How often do you and your partner butt heads and have disagreements?___
2. Are you able to get your point across during those disagreements?___
3. Do you feel like your partner listens to what you're saying when you're in a fight?___

4. How often can you guys kiss and make up after a disagreement and come to a resolution that works for both of you?___
5. Do you feel your partner is pretty good about owning up to their part of a fight when they mess up?___

Shared Meaning:

1. How much do you and your partner see eye-to-eye on the things that really matter to you?___
2. How often do you guys chat about the big stuff, like where you want to be in the future, what you believe in, or how you're managing your cash money?___
3. Do you make a point to do stuff that reflects the stuff you both care about?___
4. Do you feel like your partner really gets where you're coming from when you're talking about the important stuff?___
5. How often do you feel like you and your partner are on a shared mission, working towards something awesome together?___

Trust and Commitment:

1. How much do you trust your partner and feel like they've got your back?___

2. How often do you get those icky feelings about whether your partner is being faithful?___

3. Do you feel like your partner is really in it for the long haul, like they're fully committed to the relationship?___

4. How often do you guys make plans together and actually follow through on them?___

5. Does your partner show you they're serious about your relationship in the way they act and treat you?___

Friendship and Intimacy:

- If you scored between 1 and 3 points, you might feel like something's off between you and your partner. Maybe you're not communicating well, not getting enough time together, or just not feeling that spark anymore.
- If you scored between 4 and 5 points, things look good! You're feeling pretty connected to your partner; you enjoy spending time together which gives you the emotional and physical intimacy you need.

Suggestions for improvement

- Make time for regular date nights or activities that you both love to do. It's essential to keep the spark alive and have fun together!

- Talk to each other openly and honestly about your feelings, needs, and desires. Set aside some quality time to have deep, meaningful conversations and really listen to each other's thoughts and feelings. This can help you get closer and strengthen your relationship.
- Get creative and try new things to connect with each other emotionally and physically. Try a new hobby like rock climbing, dancing, or cooking together. The shared experience and physical activity can bring you closer and help you feel more connected.
- Experiment with different types of touch, like holding hands, hugging, or giving each other massages. This can help build physical and emotional connections and make you feel even closer.

Conflict Management:

- 1-3 points: You may struggle to communicate effectively during disagreements, feel like your needs are not being heard or understood, and/or find it difficult to come to a resolution.
- 4-5 points: You and your partner are able to communicate effectively during conflicts, listen to each other's perspectives, and work towards a mutually beneficial resolution.

Suggestions for improvement:

- Practice active listening skills, such as repeating what your partner said to show understanding.
- Avoid using blame or criticism during conflicts and instead focus on expressing your own needs and feelings.
- Try to find compromises and solutions that work for both you and your partner.

Shared Meaning:

- If you got 1-3 points, it might feel like you and your partner aren't totally on the same page regarding what you value, your goals, or your interests. Maybe it's hard to talk about important stuff, or you don't feel as connected to each other's lives as you'd like.
- But things are looking up if you got 4-5 points! You and your partner are a great match when it comes to what you care about, what you want out of life, and what you're interested in. You can talk about important things together and connect on a deep level.

Suggestions for improvement:

- If you got 1-3 points, it might help to find some common ground. Look for interests or activities that you both enjoy and can do it together. This can help you feel more connected and give you something fun to bond with.

- Try to make time to discuss your values and goals and find ways to align your individual aspirations with shared aspirations. Maybe you can work towards a common goal or find ways to support each other's dreams. This can help you feel more connected and like you're working towards something together.
- Share your life experiences and perspectives with each other. This can help you deepen your understanding of each other and connect on a more personal level. You might learn something new and exciting about your partner that you never knew before!

Trust and Commitment:

- If you got 1-3 points, it's normal to feel uncertain or have doubts sometimes. But it's important to talk to your partner about your feelings and address your concerns.

Communication is key!

- If you got 4-5 points, congratulations! It's great that you and your partner have a strong level of trust and commitment.

Remember that trust and commitment are ongoing efforts. Keep communicating openly and honestly with each other, and continue to follow through on your commitments. This can help strengthen your bond and build an even stronger foundation of trust.

Suggestions for improvement:

- Try to build trust by being open and honest with each other. Follow through on commitments and show your partner they can rely on you. When you make promises, could you do your best to keep them? This can help build trust over time.
- Remember that a strong relationship takes effort from both partners. Ensure you're both invested in the relationship and willing to work together to make it strong and healthy. When you're committed and on the same page, you're more likely to build a strong trust and mutual respect foundation.

So, if you read the self-assessment and found it helpful, here's what you can do next in a more chill way:

1. Firstly, find a quiet and distraction-free time to go through the assessment and answer each question truthfully.
2. Once you're done, calculate the average score for each area. Take note of the areas that need the

most improvement. Don't worry if some scores are low because you can always work on them.

3. After that, check out my earlier suggestions and see which would work best for you. You don't have to do everything at once, though. Just take one thing at a time and slowly work on them. Remember, Rome wasn't built in a day!

4. If you need to, talk to your partner about the results and tell them how you feel. You could also consider seeking the help of a couple therapist or counselor or participating in activities that help build a stronger relationship.

5. Lastly, improving your relationship takes time and effort, so be patient and committed. With a bit of work, you'll notice a significant improvement in your relationship satisfaction.

Now that we reach the end of this serpentine maze of Jealousy and Insecurity, let's not unfasten those seatbelts just yet! There's a sequel to this blockbuster, and we've only scratched the surface.

Make way for the celebrity of emotions, the mighty *Lord Trust* - the redwood tree in our love jungle. Its branches are the loving embrace of a sage – keeping the fort steady when insecurities go on a thunderous rampage.

You must don your most gallant gear in the upcoming chapters because we're about to morph into the protectors of love. Our holy quest to construct the Fortress of Trust, one shimmery stone at a time, in the enchanted realm of Romancia will require your utmost attention.

We'll become wordsmiths in the ballet of communication – it's like tangling with letters without tripping anyone's laces.

And behold, the towering pillars - limits and hopes - ensure the stars don't come tumbling down on those rendezvous. Amidst it all, we'll be sowing seeds of togetherness and attachment that'll sprout into beautiful sanctuaries for your love life.

Remember, it's not just about patching up a love boat; it's about raising a citadel that makes even Cupid go green. Let's get your fill in the next chapter on building a healthy, secure, and loving relationship.

3

HOW TO BUILD TRUST IN YOUR RELATIONSHIP AND KEEP IT STRONG

Hold your love boats steady because we are about to set sail on the tranquil waters of Trust Lake. In this chapter, we'll explore how trust is not just a word but the heartbeat of a thriving relationship. This chapter will explain why trust is important and how to build it in a relationship.

Imagine trust as the Golden Gate Bridge of your love life. This majestic structure doesn't pop up overnight; it's built with sturdy materials and stands tall, weathering storms. In a relationship, trust is that sturdy bridge that connects two hearts. The bricks? Communication, reliability, boundaries, and repairs!

To lay the first brick, you, as a couple, must talk. Not just everyday chit-chat but heart-to-heart conversations. Share your dreams, your fears, and your day. Listen, and I mean really listen, to your partner's words, the notes, and the symphony behind them (Marshall, 2020). This two-way street can become a highway of understanding.

Now, imagine if the Golden Gate Bridge had flimsy beams. We don't want that! Consistency and reliability are your relationship's steel beams. Show up, not just physically, but emotionally. Be the person your partner can lean on - in sunshine and thunderstorms.

Next, you will need boundaries. These are like the safety rails on the bridge. They keep you from tumbling over the edge (Gupta, 2021). Establishing what's okay and what's a no-go zone in your relationship is crucial. Respect each other's boundaries like they're sacred scrolls.

Alas, sometimes, storms can cause damage to your trust bridge. But all is not lost! Address these breaches honestly and work together like a maintenance crew. Patch up the holes, and your bridge may become stronger.

Remember, as trust blossoms, your relationship transforms. It becomes a safe haven where love flourishes, laughter echoes, and dreams take flight. Moreover, remember, trust-building is like tending a garden; it requires nurturing. If you've got the will, grab your relationship toolkit and start building.

IMPORTANCE OF TRUST

Imagine trust as an invisible, all-powerful glue that binds two souls together. It's a majestic, almost ethereal force made of confidence, safety, and reliance. When you trust someone, you take a piece of your heart in their honor. You are saying, "Here, I am giving you a treasure; please guard it with your life."

Trust is similar to leaving precious secrets in someone's hands, knowing they will cradle them gently (Gupta, 2021). It is like a delicate waltz where you close your eyes and let the rhythm guide you, certain that your partner will not let you stumble.

Let's envision a relationship as a lush, blooming garden. The flowers are love, the soil is understanding, and trust? Trust is the life-giving sunlight without which nothing thrives. Here's why trust is as vital as the sun to a garden:

1. Safety's Warm Embrace

With trust, your relationship garden becomes a sanctuary, a refuge from the storms of life. You know that, come what may, there's someone with open arms and a heart that understands.

2. Fertile Soil for Dreams

When you trust your partner, you become a dreamer and a believer (Marshall, 2020). Your aspirations find fertile soil as you dare to reach for the stars, secure in the knowledge that someone believes in you just as fiercely.

3. The Magic Potion of Freedom

Trust bestows upon your love the gift of freedom. It's like an unshackled, untethered bird soaring in the sky (Glass, 2019). When you trust, you give each other the space to be yourselves, grow, and flourish.

4. A Tapestry of Emotional Depth

As trust weaves its magic, your emotional tapestry becomes richer and more intricate. You share, laugh, and cry; sometimes, you sit silently, knowing that words are mere mortals in the empire of trust.

As guardians of love's garden, we must guard the keystone of trust with valor. For when trust shatters, the arch trembles. But worry not, for trust is also resilient. With tender care, open hearts, and hands clasped together, trust can be nurtured, mended, and held aloft as the glorious keystone of your love's majestic arch.

SIGNS THAT YOU MAY LACK TRUST IN A RELATIONSHIP

Relationships can sometimes feel like navigating a maze in the dark, especially when trust starts playing hide and seek. If you are wondering if something is happening with you, here are some signs that might mean you lack faith in your relationship.

1. Wearing an armor

Ever feel like you're walking around in an emotional suit of armor around your partner? If letting your guard down feels like lowering a drawbridge over a moat full of crocodiles, that might be a sign trust is missing from your relationship equation.

2. Being a lone sovereign

Do you often grab the reins, preferring to do everything yourself rather than delegating tasks to your partner? This do-it-yourself attitude might mean you're struggling to trust your partner's ability to care for things.

3. Silent surveillance

Do you sometimes become a social media detective, secretly monitoring your partner's activity? If your thumb often takes you on an undercover tour of their likes, comments, and posts, a trust may need more room in your relationship.

4. The enigmatic text messenger

Does your heart race at seeing their phone lighting up with a text message? It might indicate a trust issue if your imagination fires up with suspicions whenever their phone pings.

5. The ominous silence

Is your mind a disaster movie director when your partner doesn't pick up the phone? If your thoughts instantly imagine the worst-case scenarios, you might be dealing with trust problems (Marshall, 2020).

6. The unspoken desires

If you struggle to voice what you want or need, that might be a red flag indicating trust issues. If asking for what you want feels like walking a tightrope, you should look deeper into your relationship.

7. The Mistrusting Gaze

Are you often wary of your partner's interactions with friends and family? If you feel like a lone detective in a world of suspects, it could be a signal that trust is in short supply.

8. The fortress of grudges

Does your mental library hold a vast collection of grudges? If past mistakes haunt your present, it might be time to check the trust levels in your relationship.

9. The dual shadows

Ever feel like you're starting fights over things that usually wouldn't bother you? If you're throwing jabs over minor issues, it could express underlying trust issues.

10. The abyss of abandonment

Suppose the thought of abandonment is more terrifying than a roller coaster ride. In that case, it's a clear sign that trust is something you need to work on in your relationship.

Remember, it's okay to face these issues. It's the first step towards building a stronger, more trusting relationship. And you've got this, my friend!

Why is trust important in relationships?

There are several reasons why trust is pivotal for your relationship. For instance, imagine you're in a game where you must dodge flying pies. Not fun, right? That's how a relationship feels when you're constantly ducking and dodging arguments. But trust is like a magical pie-repellent (Glass, 2019). When you trust each other, the pies stop flying. The misunderstandings and squabbles take a back seat, and you can cruise through Relationship Road without constantly cleaning the pie off your face.

Trust is the key that unlocks a deeper connection in your relationship. It enables you to shift from casual conversations to profound discussions and heartfelt exchanges. It lets you openly share your aspirations, apprehensions, and even those cringe-worthy memories from childhood. The most reassuring aspect? The specific knowledge that your partner supports you and you reciprocate that support. Trust fosters a sense of security within your relationship, making it a safe haven in any storm.

Moreover, with trust, you don't have to be glued to each other. Trust gives you the freedom to do your thing and your partner to do theirs. Like, if you want to take a salsa class, and they want to join a book club, no sweat! You both get to grow and explore, and guess what? You'll have exciting stories to share at dinner. How cool is that?

Impact of Lack of Trust in a Relationship

In the realm of relationships, trust is the lighthouse that guides ships to safe shores. However, when the light of trust flickers and fades, we find ourselves adrift in murky waters. Let us look at the impact of lack of trust on a relationship.

1. Lack of Intimacy

When trust starts to wobble, the first casualty often tends to be intimacy. When we can't trust, we're reluctant to open ourselves completely, right? It's like refusing to remove a heavy coat on a hot day. We're missing out on feeling the warm sun or, in this case, the deep bond that intimacy can create.

2. Insecurity

With trust missing in action, insecurity starts to sneak in. Doubts begin to pop up like pesky, uninvited guests, and we're constantly questioning ourselves and our partners. "Are they telling the truth? Do they still love me?" And these questions, my friend, are a sure-fire recipe for feeling insecure.

3. Depression and Anxiety

Lack of trust can really mess with our heads and can leave us feeling sad or anxious. Imagine always having a dark cloud above your head, pouring down stress and worry. This can push us into depression or ramp up our anxiety levels, which isn't great, right?

4. Trouble Concentrating

Have you ever tried focusing on something when your mind buzzes with a million doubts? It's like trying to read a book at a rock concert. The constant worry and uncertainty can be a big distraction, making it tough to concentrate on other important stuff in our lives.

5. Distress

Trust issues can leave you feeling distressed. It's like having a stone in your shoe that you can't shake out. It's that constant, uncomfortable feeling that something just isn't right.

6. Fear and Loneliness

Lack of trust can bring along some unwanted companions - fear and loneliness. We might fear losing our partner, being lied to, or being hurt. It's as if we're walking on a tightrope, afraid of falling at any moment. On top of this, the isolation creeps in because we're keeping our feelings bottled up. It's like being at a party but feeling utterly alone.

In essence, trust is the harbinger of hope and unity. When trust decides to take a vacation, it can turn things upside down in a relationship. It's essential to keep trust front and center to keep the good vibes flowing and avoid these unwanted side effects.

STRATEGIES FOR BUILDING TRUST WITH YOUR PARTNER

In the landscape of love, trust is the solid foundation upon which the magnificent castle of a relationship is built. If you need to build trust in your relationship, then don't be afraid. This section will walk you through ten trust-building exercises to strengthen your love's fortifications.

1. Be Open, Acknowledge Feelings & Practice Being Vulnerable

Building trust is all about showing your true colors. Opening up, sharing feelings, and letting your guard down can feel daunting, but it's the first step towards deep connection. Remember, vulnerability is not weakness; it's courage in its purest form.

2. Assume Your Partner Has Good Intentions

Believe that your partner means well. We all make mistakes and sometimes say things we don't tell. Before jumping to conclusions, give them the benefit of the doubt. This understanding can be a strong foundation for trust.

3. Be Honest & Communicate About Key Issues in Your Relationship

Honesty is a trust superpower. When discussing issues, be candid but kind. Clear, honest communication eliminates misunderstandings and keeps the trust highway smooth.

4. Acknowledge How Past Hurts May Trigger Mistrust in the Present

Our past experiences can cloud our judgment. Recognize that an old wound may influence how you view your partner's actions. Understanding these triggers allows us to separate past hurt from present reality, paving the way for trust.

5. Listen to Your Partner's Side of the Story

Listening is just as important as talking. When your partner is sharing, be all ears. Understand their perspective before you react. Genuine listening can breed trust faster than you think!

6. Trust Your Intuition

Our gut feelings are our internal GPS. If something feels off, it probably is. At the same time, if your gut says this is right, trust it. Your intuition can be a trusty guide in your trust-building journey.

7. Practice Repair After an Argument

Arguments happen, and that's okay. What matters is what happens after. Apologize, forgive, and learn from the situation. These repairs help strengthen the trust bridge you're building.

8. Know That It Is Not Needed to Say What You Need

Trust involves understanding each other so well that words become optional at times. A look, a gesture, or a silence can speak volumes. This silent understanding can boost trust like nothing else.

9. Remember to Say "I Love You"

Three simple words: immense power. Regularly telling your partner you love them reinforces your commitment to them. This affirmation helps build a trust-filled environment.

10. Be Sure to Appreciate and Show Gratitude

Recognize and appreciate your partner's efforts. A simple thank you, or a smile can go a long way in making them feel valued. This mutual respect and gratitude are the building blocks of trust.

You can lay the bricks and mortar that fortify your love's castle by engaging in these trust-building exercises. Remember, trust-building is a marathon, not a sprint. Be patient, and watch your relationship blossom.

HOW DO WE REBUILD AFTER TRUST HAS BEEN BROKEN?

Trust, like a delicate vase, can shatter into pieces. When this happens, the path to rebuilding is often arduous. Still, with commitment and determination, the vase can be mended, sometimes becoming even more exquisite. Here, I will walk you through a step-by-step guide to breathe life into trust once again.

1. Acknowledge the break

The first step is admitting that trust has been damaged. Like acknowledging a wound before it can heal, both parties must recognize and accept the breach (Raypole, 2019). For instance, if a partner has been dishonest about finances, start by openly acknowledging the dishonesty and its impact on the relationship.

2. Express sincere apology

An apology should be sincere and devoid of excuses. Expressing regret for the actions that led to the breach of trust is crucial. A simple "I'm truly sorry for hiding my debts from you. I understand how this betrayal hurts you" can be a good beginning.

3. Create a trust-building blueprint

Develop a plan together for rebuilding trust. This should include steps the offending party should take and how the aggrieved party can contribute. For instance, if the trust was broken due to infidelity, the plan could include couples counseling, open communication about feelings, and time for healing (Raypole, 2019).

4. Set boundaries and expectations

Clear boundaries and expectations are the safety nets of trust. They provide a framework within which trust can be rebuilt. Example: Setting a boundary such as, "We must be transparent about our spending," can help restore trust in cases of financial dishonesty.

5. Maintain open communication

Keep the channels of communication wide open. Discuss feelings, fears, and progress honestly (Raypole, 2019). Example: Regularly scheduled "trust talks" where you both share your feelings about the trust-rebuilding process.

6. Consistency is key

Be consistent in your actions. The offending party should consistently adhere to the agreements made. An example can be a partner who has agreed to call when they are late coming home. It is important to do this every time without fail.

7. Seek professional guidance

Sometimes, guidance from a counselor or therapist can help mend the gaps where personal efforts fall short. A couple can decide to attend couples therapy to unearth deep-seated issues and to develop strategies for rebuilding trust.

8. Celebrate progress

Recognize and celebrate improvements, no matter how small. This reinforces positive behavior. A partner can give a dinner date, or a simple note of appreciation for consistently adhering to an agreement can be very encouraging.

9. Forgive but remember

Forgiveness is an integral part of rebuilding trust, but it's also important to remember the lessons learned (Raypole, 2019). Forgive your partner for a past mistake, but keep the experience as a reference for personal and relationship growth.

10. Nurture patience

Rebuilding trust is like growing a garden; it takes time. Be patient and allow the trust to bloom naturally. Avoid rushing to "get back to normal." Allow each other space and time to grow back into a trusting relationship.

Now that we have reached the end of yet another milestone let's look back at what we managed to discover. We found that trust is the bedrock upon which the structure of a strong relationship is built.

We also identified the warning signs that indicated the absence of trust and delved into the repercussions of this absence, including emotional distress and loneliness. Furthermore, the chapter shared the golden tenets of constructing trust, which include vulnerability, honesty, setting boundaries, and active communication.

For relationships where trust has crumbled, we explored a 10-step blueprint for mending the cracks. This journey through the landscape of trust is instrumental in fostering healthier and more fulfilling relationships.

The next chapter beckons us with open arms as we turn the page. Here, we will tread on the path of "Solid Communication in Relationships." Communication is the lifeline that keeps the heart of a relationship beating. It's the bridge that connects two souls, and when combined with trust, it's an unbeatable duo. So, please fasten your seat belts as we navigate the intriguing lanes of communication!

4

SOLID COMMUNICATION IN RELATIONSHIPS

L et us begin with a little tale about a flute and a violin.

In a quaint little village nestled between emerald mountains and a tranquil turquoise lake, there resided an elderly couple, Mr. and Mrs. Worthington. They were celebrated as the weavers of hearts and words.

One eventide, the village's council of elders invited the Worthingtons to share their secret potion. With a twinkle in his eye, Mr. Worthington unraveled the scroll of their love. "Hark, all! Let me tell you the story of two instruments. Once, a flute and a violin from different orchestras were entwined in matrimony. They screeched and squealed for years as their notes failed to blend into the music. It seemed their enigmatic sounds would forever be lost in translation."

"But, one night, as the violin wept her solitary notes, the flute halted his tune to listen. In that pause, he discovered the beautiful melancholy that caressed the strings of her heart. He then began to play, and instead of fighting against her tune, he complimented it with the soft whispers of his own."

"With every sunrise," Mr. Worthington continued, "the flute and the violin practiced their new-found harmony. They learned to recognize each other's melodies and express their songs without drowning out the others. They found that the secret of their symphony was in the waves of their strings and the wind in their reeds - in the way they communicated."

The couple ended their tale as the moon bowed to the rising sun. Young and old villagers sat under the spell of their wisdom.

Let us imagine relationships as this delicate symphony.

Where the hearts are the instruments and words are the melodies. In this chapter, we will explore how communication plays the role of the composer, crafting harmonious and enrapturing music.

We will learn to listen as the flute did, express our notes clearly as the violin, and compose melodies that resonate with those we hold dear. Our bonds will strengthen and flourish, not unlike the enchanting symphony of Mr. and

Mrs. Worthington, as we understand the depths and nuances of effective communication.

THE ROLE OF COMMUNICATION IN REDUCING OVERTHINKING

Think of your mind as a lush garden, with thoughts similar to leaves on a grand willow tree. When the winds of life blow, the leaves rustle and sometimes whirl into a frenzy. This garden then becomes one of "overthinking." With leaves spiraling uncontrollably, what if the whisper of communication remains the only way to calm these winds?

The act of communication is like a gentle whisper that caresses the leaves. By sharing our thoughts and feelings, we allow some of the leaves to fall to the ground gracefully, lightening the load on our branches.

Moreover, the garden of the mind needs sunlight to thrive. When communicating, we invite clarity into our thoughts (Lebow, 2016). We often gain new insights and perspectives by externalizing our concerns and expressing our thoughts verbally or in writing. This clarity is like sunlight, nurturing the roots of our thoughts.

In this garden, communication isn't only about letting the leaves fall; it's also about witnessing the leaves in someone else's garden. Active listening plays a vital role in reducing overthinking. When we listen to others, we often find parallels between their experiences and ours. This connection can calm the rustling leaves as we realize we are not alone in our thoughts.

IMPACTS OF LACK OF COMMUNICATION IN A RELATIONSHIP

Now that we know the role of communication in reducing overthinking let's take a look at the impact of lack of communication in a relationship.

Like a garden that thrives with care and wilts without it, relationships require nurturing through communication. When communication is lacking, an invisible wall is slowly erected between partners (Earnshaw, 2014). This wall, constructed of misunderstandings and unspoken feelings, becomes a barrier to the closeness once shared.

Moreover, a relationship without communication becomes an arid land where emotions cannot blossom. Without sharing thoughts, dreams, and worries, emotional intimacy begins to wither, leaving partners feeling estranged and alone, even when together.

Where words do not flow, doubt creeps in like a shadow at dusk. The absence of open dialogue can sow seeds of distrust and insecurity, as partners are left to speculate on each other's thoughts and motives.

Remember, trivial issues may escalate into full-blown conflicts without communication as the mediator. The lack of a safety valve to release and discuss frustrations leads to pressure buildup and, eventually, explosion.

In essence, two people in a relationship are like two rivers converging. Through communication, they can form a mighty, vibrant stream. But without it, the rivers stagnate, become murky, and cannot foster life. The personal growth that can be achieved together is stunted as individuals need to learn, share, or evolve with each other.

Lack of communication leads to an emotional vacuum. A heart that has much to say but finds no outlet begins to ache. The joy of sharing triumphs, the comfort of sharing sorrows, and the adventure of sharing dreams are all lost.

Without clear communication, the mind often becomes a breeding ground for assumptions (Earnshaw, 2014). When thoughts are not exchanged openly, partners may begin to assume the worst of each other. Now, that's when a relationship may start to feel burdened. In times like these, communication is key, dear reader. Remember, strong relationships are built after uncomfortable conversations that make both of you face your triggers in a relationship.

SIGNS OF BAD COMMUNICATION IN A RELATIONSHIP

If you are wondering whether your relationship is suffering, the following are some signs you could ponder upon.

The Silent Dinner Table

The silent dinner table is one of the first signs of bad communication (Earnshaw, 2014). Meals that used to be a time of conversation and laughter turn into a quiet, mechanical routine. If you both seem to be experts at sidestepping essential discussions, you're dancing to the rhythm of poor communication.

The Avoidance Dance

When partners consistently avoid discussions, particularly regarding issues or decisions within the relationship, it's a sign that communication has broken down. When conversations seem like a blame game, it might be time to reconsider communication styles.

The Blame Storm

When conversations frequently turn into blame games, where accusations and finger-pointing replace constructive dialogue, communication no longer serves its purpose.

The Emotional Fortress

Does sharing feelings or vulnerabilities feel like storming a castle? If so, your communication line might be heavily barricaded. Suppose one or both partners become emotionally guarded, reluctant to share feelings, or show vulnerability. In that case, it indicates a lack of open communication.

The Echo of Absence

When the absence of a partner doesn't create a ripple, when their silence goes unnoticed, the echoes of a lack of communication are ringing loudly.

Understanding the signs and consequences of the lack of communication is crucial to building bridges. Remember, the gardens of love can only be nurtured when hearts and words flow freely in the sacred dance of communication.

STRATEGIES FOR IMPROVING COMMUNICATION WITH YOUR PARTNER

Now, let's walk through some strategies to improve communication. After all, lets remember that communication is key for a relationship to thrive.

1. Cultivate Self-Awareness

Embark on a journey within and recognize your communication patterns, strengths, and weaknesses (Davin, 2022). Knowing oneself is the first step in understanding how you contribute to the conversations in your relationship.

2. Pledge for Transformation

Make a sincere promise to yourself and your partner to bring positive change to your communication. Share this commitment openly and let it serve as a guiding light for your words and actions.

3. Forge the Bonds of Responsibility

Hold yourself accountable for your part in communication. Create an alliance with your partner where you both serve as guardians, ensuring each other stays true to the commitment to change.

4. Unravel the Threads of Attachment

Your soul's tapestry is woven by the bonds formed in your early days. Comprehend how your attachment styles, forged in the cradle, impact your communication (Davin, 2022). Be empathetic to how different attachment styles can shape conversations.

5. Don the Armor of Preparedness

Instead of charging into the battleground of conflict, take a step back. After tempers cool, equip yourself with a strategy. List the challenges, designate time for conversation, exchange thoughts without interruption, and be wholly present.

6. Welcome the Winds of Change

Let your ears and heart be open to the suggestions your partner brings to the table. Understand that the path to resolution is paved with the stones of compromise and openness.

7. Embark on a Quest for Understanding

Channel your inner explorer and delve into the depths of your partner's thoughts and emotions. Be curious, ask questions, and discover the treasure trove of understanding that lies beneath the surface.

8. Establish the Gates of Respect

Create boundaries that guard the sanctity of your relationship. Express them clearly, and respect the boundaries set by your partner. This establishes a safe haven for communication.

9. Set Sail for Regular Discoveries

Make it a habit to regularly have meaningful conversations and check the state of your communication within your relationship. Set aside time to actively explore how your communication landscape is evolving and changing.

10. Reveal the Heart's Whisper

Let the soft whispers of vulnerability escape your heart. Use "I" statements to express pain, love, and dreams without casting the shadow of blame on your partner.

11. Build the Fortress of Unity

Speak with the foundation of "we" when addressing issues. Let your words be the bricks that build a united front focused on the prosperity of the relationship.

12. Revel in the Joy of Progress

As you improve your communication, take a moment to appreciate the small victories along the way. Pause and bask in the moonlight of those moments when you successfully connect and understand each other. Celebrating these milestones will energize you for the journey ahead.

13. Embrace the Grace of Patience

The waters of change can be turbulent. Be patient and grant each other the grace to grow at your own pace. Understand that the journey is as important as the destination.

WHAT TO DO WHEN THERE IS NO COMMUNICATION IN A RELATIONSHIP

In a relationship, silence can sometimes feel louder than words. If you are wondering what can be done when there's no communication in a relationship, the following strategies may help.

Assess the Landscape

When communication fields lay barren, take a moment to assess why. Is the relationship at a crossroads due to external stress or personal issues?

Embark on an Honesty Quest

In the silence, let the truth be your guiding light. Acknowledge your desires and expectations from the relationship and share them openly.

Design a Desire Blueprint

Sit down together and outline your communication goals as a team. Look for the areas where your desires and wishes align, as that's where the magic happens. Concentrate on the points you can agree on and actively work on improving your relationship.

The Power of Apology

Sometimes, a sincere apology can work like magic. It has the power to heal past wounds and revive communication that may have been buried.

When to Seek Couples Counseling for a Relationship Without Communication

If your relationship gets extremely troubled, you should seek couples counseling. After all, this is one way you can heal those wounds of the past and help foster a healthy relationship. Following are some instances in which you should consider counseling.

When Shadows Grow Long

When the shadow of silence grows so long that it seems to eclipse the relationship, it's time to consider seeking help.

When the Well is Poisoned

If communication is strained due to resentment or deeply rooted issues, a counselor can help detoxify the conversation well.

When Navigating Rough Seas

If the relationship is facing a crisis, and communication is essential in navigating through it, a counselor can serve as the guiding star.

Remember, on this journey of mending the torn tapestry, patience, love, and sometimes the guiding hand of a skilled artisan as a counselor are needed to restore the golden threads of communication.

In the tapestry of relationships, communication is the golden thread that binds hearts together. From cultivating a more profound understanding with our partners to soothing overthinking, effective communication proves to be the anchor.

RELATIONSHIP COMMUNICATION TEST

Take this test to better understand if your relationship is suffering from a lack of communication. The results will help you analyze if something is lacking and where to improve. This test is inspired by Phil (2022).

1. Do you struggle to find the right words when expressing yourself? True/False
2. Do you worry that your partner may reject you if you open up to them? True/False
3. Are you afraid to express your opinions because you think they might be wrong? True/False
4. Do you think that speaking up will only make things worse? True/False
5. Do you tend to talk more than you listen, not allowing your partner to speak? True/False
6. Do you dread having conversations with your partner? True/False
7. Do you find it hard to stop an argument once you've started? True/False
8. Do you tend to get defensive when communicating? True/False
9. Do you bring up your partner's past mistakes frequently? True/False
10. Do your actions contradict what you say? True/False
11. Do you have difficulty listening to your partner? True/False
12. Do you tend to respond to anger or insult with the same behavior? True/False
13. Do you tease your partner excessively? True/False
14. Do you avoid talking about important issues with your partner? True/False
15. Do you sometimes lie by omitting specific details? True/False

16. Do you dislike it when your partner brings up problems? True/False

17. Do you feel the need to express your complaints about your partner? True/False

18. Do you express your complaints in a heated or angry manner? True/False

19. Do you use phrases like "You always" or "You never" when discussing complaints with your partner? True/False

20. Do you avoid stating complaints to avoid hurting your partner? True/False

21. Do you avoid arguing because you think it reflects poorly on the relationship? True/False

22. Do you avoid discussing negative feelings because it makes things worse? True/False

23. Do you expect your partner to know what's bothering you without you having to express it? True/False

Analyzing the results:

Get ready for a communication checkup! With this test, your job is simple - mark 'True' or 'False' for each of the 23 statements. Once you're done, there's no pass or fail. Instead, your answers become a map, highlighting areas where your communication road might be a little bumpy. You can then decide whether you need a DIY ("Do it yourself") communication tune-up or extra help navigating relationship potholes.

Remember, relationships necessitate an intricate dance of listening, expressing with clarity, and embracing vulnerability. However, when this thread wears thin, the fabric of relationships can fray. In such instances, it's imperative to take decisive steps to mend the wear.

These steps involve breaking the silence, creating safe spaces for expression, engaging in shared interests, and sometimes seeking the guidance of a skilled couples counselor. As we navigate the labyrinthine alleys of communication, it's vital to remember that this journey is not just about speaking.

It's about weaving the tapestry with understanding, compassion, and love threads. As we close this chapter, let us prepare to dive into the depths of past shadows. In the next chapter, we will embark on a healing voyage by exploring ways to overcome past relationship traumas, allowing us to mend the sails and navigate toward calmer waters.

5

OVERCOMING PAST RELATIONSHIP TRAUMA

A calm sea never made a skilled sailor, but what if the storms are echoes from a distant past? As we steer through the boundless waters of our lives, the ghostly whispers of past relationship traumas sometimes veer us off our charted path.

In this chapter, dear reader, I will guide you on acknowledging the mysterious shipwrecks in the depths of your heart. See, the echo of past heartaches and betrayals can cast a shadow over the bountiful treasures of the present. We can set our bearings toward healthier connections by charting these treacherous waters with resilience and honesty.

Let's explore the realms of self-care, exercise, meditation, and journaling together. Keep in mind that healing is not a destination where all echoes vanish forever. It's an ongoing journey that takes us through moments of tranquility and challenges alike. We'll navigate calm waters and raging storms as we continue to grow and heal.

With a mindset of acceptance, your heart will find its way to navigate once again. Let's now delve into the depths and discover strategies to liberate our hearts from the lingering echoes of the past.

THE IMPACT OF PAST RELATIONSHIPS ON CURRENT RELATIONSHIPS

As we embark on this journey of self-discovery, it's important to recognize the echoes of transference that impact our relationships. Transference can be likened to the wind that carries embers from past relationships.

At times, our past hurts can unconsciously affect our present relationships. It's like navigating new waters yet being guided by familiar stars. The imprints of previous romances can be allies and challenges in our current journey.

Past treasures - the joy and love we once found, can make the winds favorable for new companionships. Yet, shadows of ancient storms - the heartaches, can cloud our horizons. Sometimes, we perceive a kinship between an old map and a new land, and here lies the danger. We must chart our new journeys with clear eyes, not through lenses tinted by the past. The echoes should not drown the voices of the present.

To navigate the complexities of transference, let's start by igniting the flame of self-awareness. Take the time to explore the depths of your emotions and understand where they originate from. We can better navigate our relationships' misty waters of transference by gaining clarity on their roots.

Are the tempestuous waves reacting to the present or an ancient storm roaring back to life? Remember, sometimes relationships can trigger an old wound. In fact, romantic trauma from previous journeys can manifest as an instinctual 'fight or flight' within us (Self Care Impact, 2021).

In cases of previous emotional or physical abuse, any hint of similar waters may trigger a reaction. Recognizing when you're navigating through echoes and not current storms is vital.

Now, let's unravel the cords to steer through the storms:

- If betrayal in a past relationship sets your heart into a storm of panic, anchor down and communicate your fears and needs for safety with your current partner (Self Care Impact, 2021).
- Suppose past experiences of dominance from previous co-navigators make you hesitant or uncertain about your partner's words. In that case, it's crucial to communicate your perspective openly. Together, you can explore ways to express

your opinions in a manner that doesn't disrupt the stability of your relationship. Remember, it's about finding a balance where both voices are heard and respected as you sail through the journey together.

- Sometimes, past experiences' emotional turbulence can make us anxious when conflicts arise. It's important to remind ourselves that conflicts are like ordinary winds, a natural part of any journey. By facing them together, we can navigate through without letting them capsize our relationship.
- Physical or intimate traumas are like maelstroms within. Before embarking on a new journey, anchor at a safe harbor. Heal, talk to a navigator of the soul – a therapist when the sea is calm within, set sail.

As you navigate through these echoes, always remember that your relationship is resilient and your ship is strong. The stars above will guide you along the way. Trust that by allowing your heart to be free, you and your relationship will weather the strongest winds and emerge even stronger on the other side.

14 STRATEGIES FOR OVERCOMING TRAUMA AND LETTING GO OF PAST HURTS

Breaking free from the chains of past traumas and emotions can feel like emerging from a chrysalis, ready to spread your wings and rise. Let's explore some thoughtful techniques to foster this journey of transformation:

1. Question the Comfort of Pain:

It can be tempting to take solace in familiar sorrows, wrapping them around us like a comforting blanket. But ask yourself, "Am I clinging to this pain because it's known?" Recognizing this paradox is vital, as being mired in grief can obstruct growth and the potential for joy.

2. Release Your Emotions:

Imagine your emotions as a reservoir, holding a vast amount of energy within. If we keep them bottled up for too long, it can eventually lead to an overwhelming flood. Instead, it's healthier to gradually open the sluice gates and let your feelings flow. Find diverse mediums to express yourself, whether it's through speaking, writing, art, or any other form of creative expression that resonates with you. Give yourself the freedom to release and channel your emotions in a way that feels most authentic and right.

3. Embrace Affirmations:

Elevate your spirit with the power of affirming words that act as the wind beneath your wings. Repeat empowering phrases like "I choose to let go of the past" or "I am resilient" to strengthen your mindset and fuel your determination to move forward. You'll find the inner strength to overcome challenges and soar to new heights by instilling your psyche with fortitude and positivity.

4. Cultivate Mindfulness:

1. Take charge of your thoughts and become the gatekeeper of your mind.
2. Embrace the present moment and allow yourself to experience your emotions without judgment.
3. Guide your thoughts towards a serene and accepting landscape where you can cultivate inner peace and mindfulness.

By being mindful of your thoughts and creating a positive mental environment, you'll foster a sense of tranquility and acceptance within yourself.

5. Meditate and Visualize:

1. Take some time for a meditative journey into the depths of your mind.
2. Imagine your past pain as something you can hold in your hands.

3. Acknowledge the lessons it has taught you and feel grateful for the growth it has brought into your life.

4. Let it go with love and observe as it slowly fades away. This visualization can help you find healing and freedom, enabling you to move forward with a lighter heart and a renewed sense of inner peace.

6. Practice Radical Acceptance:

Acknowledge the past as a sealed chapter in your life's narrative. You don't have to appreciate what unfolded, but accepting its inalterability allows you to flip the page and commence a fresh chapter.

7. Forgiveness - A Balm for Wounds:

The ties that bind us to past afflictions can often be forged from the weight of bitterness. To break free from these shackles, applying the healing balm of forgiveness is essential. This includes not only forgiving others who may have been involved but, equally importantly, extending forgiveness to yourself. Let go of resentments and release the burden of the past, allowing yourself to embrace inner peace and move forward with a lighter heart.

8. Engage in Inner Child and Shadow Work:

Shadow Work, a concept rooted in the theories of psychologist Carl Jung, focuses on the hidden aspects of our personality that we tend to suppress or overlook. These may include desires, feelings, or characteristics that we consider unacceptable or have been conditioned to suppress. It is vital for personal growth, self-awareness, and emotional healing to confront and integrate these facets into our consciousness. By acknowledging and embracing these aspects, we can embark on a transformative journey of self-discovery and inner healing.

Here are three illuminating techniques to start the profound journey of Shadow Work:

Ink Your Shadow:

Journaling isn't just a record of daily events. Plunge deeper. Begin by noting traits you detest in others. Often, our intense aversions reflect our own shadow. For each trait, probe if you've ever displayed similar behavior. Be unflinchingly honest. As you identify these traits within yourself, consider how you can accept or alter them constructively.

Dialogues with the Shadow:

1. Create a mental tête-à-tête with your shadow.
2. In a serene space, envision your shadow confronting you, taking a form that embodies your concealed emotions or traits.
3. Initiate a conversation, listening attentively to the responses that surface. Gratitude towards your

shadow for revealing itself is vital, as is a non-judgmental stance.

Mirror Method:

Under the dim light, gaze at your reflection in a mirror. As you ask your shadow to materialize, your face might appear to transform. This isn't a supernatural event, but your mind's way of unveiling your psyche's layers. Express thanks to your shadow and accept what you've learned with an open heart.

Shadow work can be intense and, sometimes, unsettling. Approach it with an open mind and a compassionate heart. Support from a therapist or counselor could offer beneficial guidance throughout this process. This journey leads to a more authentic, conscious, and integrated life.

9. Reconnect to Yourself:

Trauma or unhealthy relationships can estrange us from our true selves. It's crucial to re-establish this bond. Spend time doing things that bring joy and make you feel alive. Reflect on your principles, your purpose, and your aspirations. Understanding and reconnecting with your inner self is essential to liberating yourself from the past.

10. Reconnect with Your Body:

Trauma and stress often manifest in our bodies, leaving an impact. Engaging in activities like yoga, dance, or regular exercise can play a vital role in releasing emotional tension. It's important to listen to your body and be aware of its needs and signals. Nourishing yourself with healthy food, getting enough restful sleep, and practicing deep breathing exercises are simple yet powerful ways to renew your connection with your body. These practices can help restore balance and well-being, promoting a healthier mind-body connection.

11. Give Yourself Grace:

Recognize that healing is a journey, and it's essential to be gentle and patient with yourself. Allow room for mistakes, honor your emotions, and give yourself time. Celebrate even the smallest victories along the way and avoid self-criticism. Remember, healing is a process, and by granting yourself grace, you create a nurturing environment for growth and self-compassion.

12. Let Go of the Past in Relationships:

Holding onto past resentments can hinder our present relationships. Communication is the pillar here. Share your past with your partner, and be receptive to hearing theirs. Set boundaries and create new, positive shared experiences. Release the urge to control, focusing instead on building trust (Gepp, 2022).

13. Let Go of Past Mistakes and Forgive Yourself:

Understand that mistakes are an integral part of human development. Reflect on the lessons these missteps imparted. Pen a letter to yourself discussing the error and your growth since then. Practice self-forgiveness, and make peace with the fact that you can't amend the past, but you can shape your present and future.

14. Let Go of Past Trauma:

Releasing past trauma often requires a multi-faceted approach. First and foremost, it's crucial to acknowledge the trauma you've experienced. Seeking support from a therapist or counselor can be incredibly helpful. Engaging in self-care activities such as pursuing hobbies, spending time with loved ones, or practicing bodywork like massages or exercise can also contribute to healing (Nguyen, 2021).

In essence, letting go of past emotions, traumas, and mistakes is a personal journey of self-discovery, acceptance, and healing (Nguyen, 2021). It's essential to be patient with yourself, prioritize self-care, maintain open communication, and seek professional help when needed. By taking these steps, you can pave the way toward a more positive and fulfilling life.

As you employ these strategies, remember that, like the metamorphosis of a butterfly, transformation takes time. Be gentle with yourself, and embrace the journey with an open heart and an empowered spirit.

HOW TO BUILD A HEALTHY RELATIONSHIP AFTER TRAUMA?

Embarking on the path to building a healthy relationship after trauma is like voyaging into uncharted waters. The journey, although challenging, can be enriching and transformative. Remember, as a silver lining of dark clouds, healthy relationships can heal old emotional wounds while paving the way for a brighter future.

1. Healing through Relationships:

Often, we underestimate the power that human connections hold in healing our emotional scars (LMFT, 2017). A healthy relationship can act as a healing balm, gently soothing old wounds and gradually restoring the vitality of your emotional health. Acknowledging this potential is your first step towards embarking on the healing journey.

2. Shattering the Crystal Castles: Tackling Unrealistic Standards:

In the wake of trauma, we often create crystal castles of unrealistic standards for ourselves. These can be as burdensome as carrying a mountain on your back. Reflect on these self-imposed expectations, and allow yourself to demolish these crystal fortresses. Remember, it's okay to be a work in progress; every masterpiece starts as a rough sketch.

3. Exploring the Abyss:

Our relationships often hold more depth than the eye can see. Dive into the depths of your current relationships and explore the hidden layers (LMFT, 2017). Recognize the emotional support, the shared laughter, and even the shared tears that strengthen your bonds. As you venture deeper, you'll often discover hidden treasures of strength and resilience that you were unaware of.

4. The Gift of Feedback:

Empowering Your Partner Feedback is a gift, a mirror that allows us to see ourselves from another's perspective. Empower your partner to give you this mirror. Let them share their observations, their concerns, and their praises. This mutual exchange can build a bridge of understanding and cooperation, fortifying your relationship.

5. Own Your Journey:

Taking Responsibility for Healing. Your healing journey is your own, a personal pilgrimage that you must embark on (Cindy, 2023). Owning this journey means acknowledging your pain, fears, and aspirations. It also means taking action—whether it's seeking professional help, practicing self-care, or establishing healthy coping mechanisms. Remember, while others can walk with you, only you can tread the path to your healing.

6. Understanding Your Echoes:

Trauma has a voice, an echo that resounds in our minds long after the event has passed. Learn to recognize this echo when it whispers in your reactions, fears, and triggers. Understanding when you're in a trauma response is like having a compass; it helps navigate emotional upheavals and paves the way for better emotional regulation.

Imagine the roots of trust reaching deep into the ground, finding strength in open communication and firm boundaries. As you tenderly water this sapling with compassion for yourself and your partner, witness how it blossoms into a magnificent tree that provides shade and comfort on life's journey.

See, embarking on the journey of fostering a wholesome relationship after experiencing trauma necessitates compassion and gentleness. Here are 10 heartfelt tips to assist you in cultivating a nurturing bond with your partner. Think of these tips as gentle whispers from the wind, guiding you toward a profound connection.

1. **Be Brave in Your Vulnerability**: Open your heart and share your inner world with your partner. When you express yourself authentically, you allow them to truly understand your thoughts and feelings. It is through this genuine connection that intimacy blossoms and feelings of isolation diminish. By creating a space of vulnerability

and openness, you nurture a deeper bond with your partner and cultivate a stronger sense of togetherness.

2. **Allow Your Partner Their Journey**: Be an empathetic listener, and avoid trying to fix or change your partner (Brickel et al., 2017). Support them in finding their own paths and solutions, walking beside them as companions, not saviors.

3. **Hold Back on Personalizing**: Recognize that sometimes your partner's reactions might be related to their own struggles and not about you. This realization can help maintain harmony, preventing misunderstandings.

4. **Banish Assumptions**: Instead of assuming what your partner might be thinking or feeling, gently ask them. Phrases like "I am curious if you feel this way..." or "Can you help me understand what you are thinking?" pave the way for honest communication.

5. **Hone Your Communication Skills**: Express your emotions and needs openly. If you need a listening ear, voice that. (Cindy, 2023). Learning and employing effective communication strategies can be vital in connecting deeply with your partner.

6. **Embrace Authenticity and Honesty**: Being authentic with yourself is a profound act of self-love. Share openly and honestly with your partner, engaging in tough conversations with tact and grace.

7. **Discover and Pursue Your Passion**: Engage in activities that invigorate your spirit. As you discover what animates you, you will not only progress in your healing journey but also draw others towards your vibrant energy, including your partner.

8. **Nurture Your Spiritual Side**: Delve into your belief system and what grounds you. Whether it's a higher power, nature, or a set of values, nurturing your spiritual side can strengthen your relationship with yourself, reflecting positively on your partnership (Cindy, 2023).

9. **Find Your Tribe**: Joining support groups or communities where people share everyday experiences or interests can be life-changing. You can reduce feelings of isolation through relatable stories and shared experiences while learning how to cultivate relationships.

10. **Seek Counseling if Needed**: As an individual or a couple, engaging in therapy can be a safe space to explore and address issues that might be challenging to discuss otherwise. A therapist can guide you through improving communication and deepening intimacy.

Now that we have walked through the terrains of navigating your emotions let's look at some natural ways to deal with anxiety. These will help you in relaxing your body and mind.

It's Not Just You!

"Don't brood. Get on with living and loving. You don't have forever."

— LEO BUSCAGLIA

You'd be surprised by how many people fall prey to overthinking when it comes to relationships. I know it feels like it's only your mind that does these crazy loops – from the outside, it often seems like everyone else has it sussed.

Trust me... They do not.

Being human doesn't come with a guidebook, but it does come with a rollercoaster of powerful emotions that we have to figure out and work through – and when you add other people and their emotions into the mix, it's no wonder that relationships are confusing.

What I'm trying to say is that you're not the only one trying to get a handle on your relationship anxiety. There are a lot of other people out there looking for the same guidance... and I'd like to take this opportunity to ask for your help in making sure they find it.

I've been through my own fair share of relationship worries, and I know how much my overthinking has contributed to my problems over the years. I wrote this book because I'm passionate about helping other people avoid the relationship stress that overthinking brings. Relationships should be a joy, and I want to help as many people as I can to experience that joy... without the over-thinking. And that's where you come in!

By leaving a review of this book on Amazon, you'll not show fellow overthinkers that there are things they can do to calm their anxious minds – and you'll show them exactly where they can find the help they're looking for.

Simply by letting other readers know how this book has helped you and a little about what they can find inside, you'll give them clear directions toward the help they're seeking.

Thank you so much for your support. You're going to make an incredible difference to someone else's life.

6

NATURAL WAYS TO DEAL WITH ANXIETY AND BOOST YOUR RELATIONSHIP AND BODY

In this chapter, we set sail on a journey towards harmony - a harmony that melds our inner landscapes with the outer tapestry of our lives. We often find ourselves entangled in the tendrils of anxiety, which can cast shadows not only on our relationships but also on the very temple that houses our spirit – our body.

But what if we were to seek solace in the arms of Mother Nature, with an arsenal of her gifts at our disposal? The echoes of modern life reverberate with the clamor of stress and anxiety.

Navigating these turbulent waters requires not just fortitude but a compass that points us towards a more serene and healthful horizon. In this chapter, I will guide you to embracing the natural embrace of healing and wellness. These unearthing tools are potent and imbued with nature's gentle touch.

WHAT IS ANXIETY?

In the labyrinth of human emotions, anxiety often emerges as an all-too-familiar companion. To discern its influence on our relationships, we must first unravel what anxiety entails.

Anxiety is a natural response to stress or perceived threats (Will Meek, 2019). Imagine standing at the edge of a cliff; your heart races, your palms sweat, and a wave of alertness washes over you.

This reaction primes you for quick thinking and action. Anxiety can be a beneficial ally in moderate doses that helps us stay focused and make necessary decisions. However, like a fire that burns too fiercely, excessive anxiety can be consuming.

When anxiety swells beyond its functional purpose, it becomes like a turbulent sea, ever-churning with worry, nervousness, and apprehension about the future. Sometimes, these feelings become so overpowering that they interfere with everyday life (Will Meek, 2019). This heightened state can be an isolated incident or, in some cases, "Generalized Anxiety Disorder," a chronic condition.

Now, let us delve into how this perturbation in our internal world affects the landscape of our relationships.

Communication Drought: Anxiety can transform the vibrant oasis of communication into a desolate desert. The unnerving whispers of worry may lead individuals to crawl into the safety of their shells, where words are scarce.

Distorted Perception: Individuals with anxiety may have trouble having clarity of judgments. Anxiety can paint perceptions in murky shades, often bending simple phrases or actions into twisted interpretations; we call that "overthinking." The casual jest of a loved one could easily be misread as a harsh barb or a dark omen.

Emotional Exhaustion: Constant worry can feel like a relentless race, draining the emotional energy from you. This emotional fatigue may result in a prickly temper or a struggle to stay grounded in relationships, weaving an invisible chasm between lovers.

Dependency or Isolation: Anxiety can push a person into a wild pendulum swing between dependency and isolation. On one side, there's an intense craving for reassurance and support from their partner. At the same time, on the other, the fear of judgment or misunderstanding sends them hurtling toward isolation. Does that sound familiar?

Physical Intimacy: When we feel overwhelmed or anxious, it can dampen our desire and make physical intimacy feel like a difficult task rather than a passionate expression of love. Anxiety can impact the warmth and closeness we experience during intimate moments with our partner. It's essential to address these feelings and find ways to create a more comfortable and loving atmosphere to nurture our connection.

Hyper-vigilance in Relationship: Sometimes, people may feel anxious and constantly overthink their relationship, looking for hidden meanings or anticipating problems that might arise. This constant vigilance can overwhelm everyone involved, creating a sense of oppression within the relationship. It's important to find ways to ease these feelings and foster an environment of trust and open communication to alleviate unnecessary stress and strain.

To nurture the gardens of our relationships, we must tend to the weeds of anxiety that lead to overthinking. Understanding its nature and acknowledging its presence is the first step. One can learn to manage anxiety through open communication, professional help, self-help techniques, and sometimes medication.

Healthy relationships are like a duet, where both individuals contribute to the melody. When anxiety tries to silence the notes, recognizing it and seeking harmony through understanding and support can revive the symphony.

SYMPTOMS OF ANXIETY

Now, let's take a look at the symptoms associated with anxiety. These will help you discern if you face the same.

1. Muscle Tension: Living with chronic anxiety can feel like carrying an invisible heavy load everywhere you go. Always on guard, your body tightens its muscles in preparation for a potential "fight or flight" situation (Mind, 2021). It's like having a sneaky thief that keeps your muscles perpetually clenched, stealing away your ease and comfort.

But hey, remember that you're not alone in this journey. Together, we'll find ways to lighten that burden and loosen those tense muscles.

2. Chest Tightness: For many people experiencing anxiety, chest tightness can feel like a pounding heart trapped in a vice grip (Mind, 2021). It can be so overwhelming that it's sometimes mistaken for a heart attack. Try practicing the deep breathing and Grounding Techniques we learned in Chapter One to find relief. These exercises help ease the tension and provide a sense of calm during anxious moments. Remember, taking care of yourself and finding healthy ways to manage anxiety is essential.

3. Heart Palpitations: Anxiety often races the heart, making it flutter like a bird trapped in a cage. These palpitations can be frightening, exacerbating anxiety (Mind, 2021). Understanding that palpitations can be a normal response to stress and focusing on calming the mind can help ease the heart's frenetic pace.

4. High Blood Pressure: Imagine your body as a finely tuned machine, ready to face any challenge that comes its way. But when stress creeps in, it's like a power surge that redirects the flow of life within you.

In its wisdom, your body diverts blood to essential organs, preparing you for the fight-or-flight response. However, this intricate dance can have consequences for your blood pressure. Therefore, monitoring blood pressure and engaging in stress reduction activities is essential.

Here are three stress reduction activities:

1. Meditation: Meditation can help calm the mind, reduce anxiety, and promote relaxation.
2. Exercise: Engaging in regular physical activity, such as walking, jogging, or yoga, can release endorphins and help relieve stress.
3. Listening to Music: Listening to soothing music or your favorite tunes can have a calming effect and lower stress levels.

5. Insomnia: Oh, the tireless mind, constantly worrying and refusing to take a break, even when it's bedtime! This hyperarousal state can make falling asleep or staying asleep a real challenge. It's like anxiety brings along its unwanted friend, insomnia. But fear not, my friend! We've got some tips to help you combat anxiety-related insomnia.

First, let's create a sleep-friendly environment that feels cozy and calming. Dim the lights, keep distractions at bay, and add some comfy pillows to snuggle with. Second, establish a regular sleep routine. Try going to bed and waking up simultaneously each day, even on weekends. This will help regulate your body's internal clock and make falling asleep easier; with some patience and adjustments, you'll beat insomnia and conquer those restless nights!

6. Digestive Problems: Like a second mind, your gut mirrors your emotional weather, turning anxious rumblings into real-life indigestion, nausea, or irregular bowel movements. By adopting a balanced diet and relaxation rituals, you can appease this sensitive organ even amidst anxiety's storm.

7. Panic Attacks: Think of panic attacks as anxiety's dramatic symphony, with dread crescendos marked by physical tremors, excessive sweating, and ominous forebodings. But by learning the rhythm of these peaks — recognizing triggers and mastering Grounding Techniques — you can orchestrate your calming counterpoints.

8. Irritability: When anxiety stirs up a storm in your mind, even the smallest things can trigger a stormy response. But don't worry my dear friend; being aware of this susceptibility to irritability and engaging in soothing activities can help you sail through calmer waters.

9. Difficulty Concentrating: Picture anxiety as a mental jamboree, causing chaos in your mind's symphony and making it hard to focus. But there's a way to find harmony again. Try breaking tasks into smaller, manageable pieces and allocate specific' focus slots' for each one. By doing this, you can tune out the clamor of anxiety and regain your focus and productivity. It's like finding the right notes in the midst of a noisy orchestra, and with a bit of practice, you'll be back in tune and in control.

10. Restlessness: Anxiety can create a sense of constant unease that may make you feel fidgety, with internal turmoil physically taking a toll on you. But don't let it overwhelm you! Instead, channel that jittery energy into physical activities to bring back a sense of calm and tranquility.

11. Sweating: Anxiety can trigger your body's survival instinct, causing you to produce more sweat as a way to cool down. Don't worry; it's a natural response! Embrace it by choosing breathable clothes that will help you stay comfortable. Also, remember to stay well-hydrated to support your body during these moments. Hydration can play a crucial role in managing the effects of anxiety. With the proper clothing and fluids, you'll be better equipped to easily tackle those anxious moments.

12. Anxiousness: When unrelenting dread, anxiety's signature, threatens to immobilize you, there's a way to find relief. Embrace the power of mindfulness and Grounding Techniques to clear those looming clouds and bring you back to the safety of the present moment. You can regain control and ease by staying focused on the here and now, allowing those anxieties to dissipate.

13. Inability to Socialize: Anxiety can create invisible barriers that overwhelm social interactions. But fear not, my friend! You can gradually chip away at these walls by taking small steps and confiding in trusted allies. As you do so, you'll find that socializing becomes less like breaching a fortress and more like connecting with others in a genuine and fulfilling way. Remember, you don't have to face it all at once; little by little, you'll build the confidence and comfort you need to easily navigate social situations.

Natural Ways to Reduce Anxiety

There are several natural ways to reduce anxiety, and I'd be happy to share them with you. Let's explore some of these methods together.

1-Engage in Regular Physical Activity

Elevating your wellness and state of being could be as effortless as inviting steady physical activities into your everyday dance of life. Like a magic potion, exercise not only enhances the lullaby of sleep and infuses energy but also eases the knots of stress and tension.

Gentle activities like yoga and tai chi shine brightly for those wrestling with the shadow of anxiety. Their tranquil rhythms and the soothing ballet of deep breaths are like a gentle rain on the parched soil of stress and tense muscles.

Studies whisper tales of yoga's victories, showcasing significant declines in the stormy symptoms of stress and anxiety. Besides, yoga can be the master key to tinkering with your brain's chemistry, altering elements like GABA levels, and modulating the symphony of neural activity (McDermott, 2021).

But if yoga doesn't strike a chord with you, worry not. The world of physical activities is as vast as the ocean. Whether it's the rhythmic run, a peaceful stroll amid nature's artwork, lifting weights, or swirling in a dance, each has the potential to soothe your mind and body. It's crucial to pick an activity that you find joyful and can pledge a long-term friendship with.

2-Reconsider Drinking as a coping mechanism

When anxiety knocks, you may be tempted to drown it in a glass of alcohol. Yet, this fleeting respite may fan anxiety's flames. There's a notable bond between anxiety and alcohol. Trimming down your alcohol intake could be a powerful tool in mitigating anxiety's dark clouds.

Binge drinking meddles with your brain's neurotransmitters, escalating anxiety and casting a shadow over your mental health. But the silver lining is that curtailing alcohol can restore balance and curb anxiety.

The journey to reducing alcohol may initially feel like a rocky climb, potentially stirring anxiety. Still, the view from the peak — the long-term benefits — is breathtaking. Plus, alcohol can sabotage your sleep — a vital ally in your battle against anxiety. Therefore, seeking healthier coping strategies is wise, prioritizing your mental and physical well-being.

3-Avoid Smoking

For many, the flicker of a cigarette is like a lighthouse in a storm. But like alcohol, this beacon can lead you into deeper, troubled waters, exacerbating anxiety over time.

The dance between smoking and anxiety can morph into a dangerous whirl, where anxiety fuels smoking, sparking even more anxiety (McDermott, 2021). Replacing this frantic tango with healthier rhythms like exercising, meditating, or therapy is crucial.

While these alternatives might take time to show their magic, they promise lasting rewards for your mental and physical health. Quitting smoking can also brighten your mood and give you a sense of accomplishment and a surplus of energy to wrestle with stress. Plus, it has a delightful side effect of fresher clothes and hair, better skin and healthier lungs!

4-Reduce Your Caffeine Consumption

Here's something interesting to consider - that beloved cup of caffeine you enjoy could contribute to your anxiety, especially if you're dealing with chronic anxiety. Caffeine can sometimes add to restlessness and jitteriness, making anxiety tremors feel more pronounced (Dr. Josh, 2018).

If you're working on strategies to manage anxiety, it might be worth taking a closer look at your caffeine intake. But don't fret! There's a whole universe of delightful and healthy caffeine alternatives out there. From soothing herbal teas to good ol' hydrator water, you have plenty of options to choose from. So, if you're ready to explore a world of flavors and benefits, let's find the perfect caffeine-free drinks to keep you calm and refreshed. Cheers to better choices and a more relaxed you!

- **Herbal Teas**: Many herbal teas exist without caffeine and can be incredibly calming. Some renowned options encompass chamomile, peppermint, and lavender tea.

- **Decaffeinated Coffee or Tea**: If you're fond of the flavors of coffee or tea but aspire to diminish caffeine intake, you can opt for decaffeinated variants of your preferred beverages.
- **Water**: Maintaining hydration is vital for holistic well-being and can make you feel more awake and lively. Additionally, sipping water can serve as an excellent, brief respite to refocus when anxiety begins to creep in.
- **Fruit Juices or Smoothies**: A glass of freshly pressed juice or a nutritious smoothie concocted with an assortment of fruits and vegetables can be an excellent means to invigorate yourself without relying on caffeine.
- **Golden Milk or Turmeric Latte**: Golden milk, sometimes called turmeric latte, is a delightful and comforting beverage prepared with a blend of turmeric, ginger, and assorted spices. This concoction is known for its ability to curb inflammation and foster a sense of calm. It's essential to remember that individuals have varied reactions to caffeine; therefore, discovering what suits you best is crucial. Feel free to sample diverse alternatives until you identify what is enjoyable and beneficial for your well-being.

5-Make Quality Sleep your Top Priority

Sleep, the secret elixir of mental health, has been the chorus of scientific research over and over. However, like a hidden treasure, many still fail to find it. According to a 2012 survey, almost a third of adults were caught in the quicksand of fewer than six hours of sleep per night.

Like a wise old sage, the CDC encourages adults to venture for 7 to 9 hours of sleep each day. It might sound like climbing a mountain, but it is a golden ticket to comprehensive health and wellness. So, what bread-crumbs can we follow to make "sleep" our trusty companion and recharge our body batteries?

Here are a few practical guidelines for emphasizing sleep:

- **Wait for Sleepiness:** The perfect time to snuggle under your covers is when you're exhausted. If you're not sleepy yet, finding sleep can be as tricky as finding a needle in a haystack. So, save your trip to dreamland until you're yawning and ready.
- **Create a Sleep-Only Sanctuary:** Keep your bed a kingdom of dreams. Reading, watching TV, or scrolling through your phone can turn your brain into a party, making sleep a gate-crasher. So, keep your bed in a VIP zone for sleep only.
- **Get Out of Bed If Sleep Eludes You:** Can't catch any Z's? Don't roll around in frustration. Get up and do something quiet until sleepiness tiptoes

back. Don't worry; it always will (especially if you start studying!).

- **Evade Sleep Saboteurs**: Watch out for sleep's arch-nemeses. Caffeine, big meals, and nicotine are like alarm clocks to your body if consumed too close to bedtime. They can steal away your precious sleep.

- **Optimize Your Sleep Environment**: Turn your bedroom into a haven of relaxation. Keeping it as dark and cool as a quiet night can welcome a peaceful slumber.

- **Empty Your Mind:** Pour your thoughts and feelings onto paper before bed. This can help clear your mind's desk and reduce worries, making it the perfect time to keep a 'thankfulness diary".

- **Establish a Consistent Bedtime:** Set your sleep schedule like clockwork. Going to bed at the same time every night is like giving your body's internal clock a roadmap. This helps make falling asleep as easy as closing your eyes.

You can establish a solid foundation by prioritizing and valuing sleep while incorporating the strategies we discussed earlier. This foundation will not only lead to better sleep but also result in improved mental and physical performance. So, let's start acting on those important tips today to build a strong base for a healthier and more vibrant you!

6-Engage in Meditation and Embrace Mindfulness

Meditation is like a voyage into the vast seas of mindfulness and heightened awareness. By boarding the ship of meditation, the goal is to sharpen the skill to be fully in the now, to peer into our own thoughts and emotions without judgment, without clinging.

Science unfurls a treasure map showing how regular meditation can shower mental and physical health benefits like the rain nurtures a parched land. It tames the wild beasts of stress and anxiety, enhances the serenity of sleep, and fosters and moves down to the toes, like the foot of a valley.

Imagine tracing the roadmap of your body, identifying areas of tension, and gently releasing it.

Chakra Meditation: It's about navigating your attention towards the chakras or energy centers of the body. The goal is to energize and balance these chakras through visualization and deep breathing exercises. You might imagine radiant discs of light rotating at each chakra point, starting from the crown of the head down to the base of the spine.

Zen Meditation: Known as Zazen, it's like sitting on a peaceful island, focusing on your breath or a koan (a philosophical puzzle). Picture yourself seated on a soft cushion, absorbed in the rhythm of your breath.

Insight Meditation: Also called Vipassana meditation, it invites you to a garden of contentment and joy.

Mindfulness Meditation: This path requires anchoring your ship in the harbor of the present, observing thoughts and feelings without casting judgment, much like a silent observer on a busy street. Focus on the ebb and flow of your breath, like the tide at sea.

Transcendental Meditation: This approach is like a lullaby, a repeated mantra that calms the tumultuous sea of the mind, leading to tranquil waters. Mantras like "Om" or "So Hum" are often used as oars to row you into this calm.

Loving-kindness Meditation: Known as Metta Meditation, it's akin to beaming out a lighthouse of love, compassion, and positivity, reaching not just yourself but extending to family, friends, and even strangers. You might silently echo affirmations like "May I find happiness, may I be healthy, may I experience peace," or use the name of the person that you desire to extend your loving-kindness.

Body Scan Meditation: This practice invites you on a voyage across your body, starting from the head, like a mountaintop, and diving deep into the ocean of your breath and bodily sensations. The goal is to unearth profound insights into the transient and interconnected nature of all phenomena. For instance, you might focus on the rush of sensations as the breath courses through your nostrils, recognizing the fleeting life of each breath.

Yogic Sleep: Yoga Nidra, translating to yogic sleep, is akin to floating in a gentle river of relaxation directed by the current of guided meditation. Imagine each body part sinking softly into the earth, releasing tension.

Sonic Immersion Meditation: Like bathing in a river of sound, this involves immersing oneself in various sounds to induce relaxation and wash away stress. Picture yourself absorbed in the echoes of a singing bowl, riding the wave of its resonance as it fades away.

Mindful Ambulation: Walking meditation is a stroll in the park of mindfulness. This involves consciously feeling the textures of each step and keenly observing the beauty of your surroundings. You might imagine walking barefoot on a grass carpet, attentive to its texture under your feet.

Realize that meditation is a vast galaxy with countless stars. There is no definitive "right" star. It's a journey to explore different stars, to find the one that resonates with your cosmic rhythm and fosters a sense of tranquility, focus, and presence in your universe.

7-Nutritious Diet

Just as the sun and rain nurture the earth, a nutritious diet is the sunlight and rainfall for our physical and mental well-being. Feeding your body with the proper nutrients can tinker with your brain chemistry, influencing your emotions and mood like a puppeteer controls a puppet.

A diverse menu of nutrient-rich foods is vital to a wholesome diet. Imagine filling your plate with a rainbow of fruits and vegetables, whole grains, lean proteins, and healthy fats. These foods are like tiny powerhouses packed with vitamins and minerals essential for the smooth running of your body and supporting brain health.

What we eat can significantly impact how we feel, especially regarding anxiety and stress. Consuming a diet high in processed foods, sugars, and unhealthy fats can be like pouring acid rain on our health. These choices can lead to fluctuating blood sugar levels, trigger inflammation, and upset the balance in our bodies, making anxiety symptoms even more intense.

On the flip side, we can nurture our bodies and minds by making healthier dietary choices. Choosing nutritious and balanced meals can help keep our blood sugar stable, reduce inflammation, and promote overall well-being. So, let's aim for a diet that supports us in feeling our best and keeps those anxiety fires in check.

Maintaining a diet full of clean and nutritious foods is like laying bricks of physical and mental health. Including natural, nutrient-dense foods in your daily meals is like adding fuel to your health. This balanced diet is key to unlocking how you feel. Aim for a balanced diet that enriches both your body and mind.

If your goal is to assuage anxiety symptoms through diet, make sure to include foods rich in nutrients like vitamin B, magnesium, calcium, and omega-3 fatty acids.

Below are some delicious and healthy choices for your food rainbow:

- Omega-3 fatty acid-rich fish like salmon, mackerel, and tuna.
- Lean protein sources like grass-fed beef or organic chicken.
- Nutritional yeast for a boost of B vitamins.
- Eggs, the B vitamins storehouse.
- A bouquet of leafy greens like spinach and kale.
- A basket of fresh vegetables like celery and broccoli.
- Fresh fruits like blueberries and bananas.
- Mineral-rich sea vegetables.
- Healthy fats like avocado, coconut oil, and olive oil.
- Protein-rich beans like black beans and chickpeas.
- Magnesium and B vitamins-rich lentils and peas.
- Healthy fat and magnesium-rich nuts like walnuts and almonds.
- Omega-3 fatty acid-rich seeds like flax seeds and chia seeds.

- Fiber and magnesium-rich whole grains like farro and quinoa.

Integrating these nutrient-dense foods into your diet can foster mental well-being and manage anxiety. Like choosing the right tools to build a house, picking the right foods is a step towards constructing a healthier you.

8-Steer Clear of Sugary and Processed Foods

Let me tell you a little story about how food choices impact our well-being:

Once upon a time, there was a person who loved sweet treats and processed snacks. They couldn't resist indulging in sugary delights all the time. Little did they know that this diet was like pouring fuel on the fire of inflammation and oxidative stress, paving the way for potential health issues like diabetes, heart disease, and even cancer. Yikes!

But then, they decided to make a change. They realized that what they ate significantly influenced their mental health, too. All those sugary and processed foods threw their gut microbiome off balance, affecting their mood and cognition. It was like riding a rollercoaster of blood sugar levels, leading to fatigue and a foggy mind. Not exactly the happy and focused life they wanted.

So, they shifted gears and embraced a diet rich in whole foods - plenty of fruits, veggies, lean proteins, and healthy fats. Do you know what happened? Their body and brain thanked them! These nutrient-packed foods provide all the crucial vitamins, minerals, and antioxidants needed for peak performance. They felt stronger, sharper, and even shielded against diseases. It was like a magical transformation!

And here's the moral of the story: for peak wellness and remarkable health benefits, prioritize nutrient-rich foods and cut back on sugary and processed treats. Those small diet tweaks snowball into an incredible difference over time. So, let's nourish ourselves with the best food choices and watch as we become the heroes of our own wellness journey!

Picture this delightful scene: a cozy kitchen filled with love and laughter, where a couple stands side by side, hand in hand, preparing a delicious meal together. As they chop, sauté, and savor the aroma of fresh ingredients, something magical happens. Amidst the clinks of utensils and shared smiles, they connect on a deeper level. Cooking together becomes a sweet dance of collaboration, trust, and creativity. It's a beautiful journey of discovering each other's tastes, preferences, and culinary dreams. This shared experience not only nourishes their bodies but also nourishes their hearts, building a bond that's as strong as the flavors they create. In the kitchen, they learn to communicate, compromise, and appreciate the simple joys of life. In these precious moments of togetherness, their relationship flourishes as they realize that preparing home-cooked meals is more than just filling their plates; it's filling their hearts with love and joy.

9-Engage in Deep Breathing Exercises

Let me share a fantastic stress-busting secret with you: deep breathing exercises! It's a simple yet powerful tool to fight stress and overthinking. Do you know how stress and anxiety can make our breathing rapid and shallow? Well, deep breathing comes to the rescue! It calms our racing hearts, soothes sweaty palms, and eases those tense muscles. How cool is that?

But wait, there's more! Deep breathing also helps us stay present and mindful, stopping that overthinking cycle in its tracks. All you have to do is focus on the beautiful flow of your breath, and voila! You're anchored in the present moment, feeling that tranquil serenity wash over you.

So, next time stress tries to sneak up on you, remember this handy trick: take a moment, take a deep breath, and let serenity and well-being fill you up.

10-Experiment with Aromatherapy:

This is a wonderful way to bring tranquility and relaxation into your life: aromatherapy! It's like an escape to a serene oasis, all with the help of plant-derived essential oils.

And guess what? Using a diffuser, you can easily make it a part of your daily routine. Just add a few drops of your favorite essential oil, and ta-da! The whole room gets filled with that calming and soothing scent.

But wait, there's more fun to be had! You can explore so many other ways to enjoy aromatherapy. How about making your own aromatherapy mist or adding essential oils to your bath? The possibilities are endless! It's like crafting your personal haven of peace right at home.

So, give it a try, my friend, and see how this little aromatherapy adventure brings relaxation and bliss into your life. You totally deserve it! Take a deep breath, enjoy the calming scents, and let all that stress and anxiety melt away.

Suppose you're interested in exploring the world of essential oils to ease anxiety. In that case, I've got some terrific suggestions from McDermott (2021). These magical oils have a reputation for doing wonders in calming those anxious nerves. Ready to discover them?

- **Lavender**: This essential oil, known for its soothing properties, is like a warm hug for your senses. It can help you relax and unwind, making it a great ally against anxiety.
- **Chamomile:** Just like a cup of chamomile tea, chamomile essential oil has a calming effect too.

It's like a gentle lullaby for your mind, helping you find peace and tranquility.

- **Ylang Ylang**: This exotic oil has a sweet and floral scent that can transport you to a tropical paradise. It's a real mood booster, reducing anxiety and promoting a sense of joy.
- **Bergamot:** Like a burst of sunshine, bergamot essential oil can lift your spirits and chase away anxiety. Its citrusy aroma is simply delightful!

So, go ahead and give these essential oils a try. They are the natural remedy you've been looking for to embrace a calmer and more blissful life. Enjoy the journey!

Indulge in a cup of chamomile tea. Let's explore some natural remedies to manage anxiety and bring harmony to our lives.

First up, we have the lovely chamomile tea! This soothing brew is famous for its calming properties and can work wonders in promoting relaxation and easing overthinking. Incorporating it into your routine is as easy as taking a moment to savor a comforting cup. It's like a little daily dose of tranquility that also improves sleep quality. Cheers to that!

Next, let's talk about the power of supplements. Just like vigilant conductors of our emotions, some natural supplements can strike the right chords and enhance our moods. Herbs and supplements can be like helpful friends, supporting us in managing anxiety and taking charge of our well-being. They boost neurotransmitters like serotonin and dopamine, which are essential for regulating our mood and keeping us balanced.

My dear friend, as we reach the end of this chapter, let's take a moment to reflect on the beautiful lesson it holds. Managing anxiety and nurturing healthier relationships go hand in hand. Still, embracing a natural approach that addresses our mind, body, and soul as one whole is essential.

You see, the solution for overthinking in relationships is more than just a quick fix or a band-aid. It's about delving deep, going to the root of the problem, and bringing a cure to every single part of our being. By incorporating natural remedies like meditation, deep breathing, supplements, a balanced diet, and regular exercise, we create a harmonious symphony within ourselves.

Remember, my friend, you are a magnificent whole, and caring for your mind, body, and soul is the key to a fulfilling and meaningful existence. So, let's take action! Embrace the lessons you've learned and apply them with kindness and dedication.

The journey towards a healthier and more fulfilling life starts with us, and we have the power to make it happen. So, let's take these steps with love, compassion, and determination.

And here comes the exciting part! In the next chapter, we'll venture into the art of mindfulness. It's all about cultivating present-moment awareness, and you know what that means? We'll be equipped with fantastic techniques to manage those pesky thoughts and foster well-being. It's like embarking on a journey of self-discovery and transformation! Are you ready for the adventure?

So, let's embrace these natural strategies together and create a symphony of peace and joy in our lives. Get ready to thrive with mindfulness and find that inner serenity you deserve. Let's go!

7

MINDFULNESS TECHNIQUES FOR BREAKING FREE FROM OVERTHINKING

Now that we have walked through the realm of overthinking and how it affects relationships, let's delve into the transformative power of mindfulness. This little bird can help you break free from the grip of overthinking.

Overthinking can consume our minds, leading to stress, anxiety, and a sense of being disconnected from the present moment. By embracing mindfulness techniques, we can gain control over our thoughts, find inner peace, and live a more fulfilling life.

THE POWER OF MINDFULNESS

Imagine sitting by a peaceful river, watching the water flow gently. Your mind is like a river, constantly moving, full of thoughts and emotions. Now, mindfulness is like becoming the observer of that river, simply watching without judgment or trying to control it.

With mindfulness, you gently focus on the present moment, soaking in everything around you - your thoughts, emotions, bodily sensations, and the world around you. It's like being fully present without getting swept away by the river of ideas.

This heightened awareness lets you see your experiences clearly and accept them just as they are. It's like having a clear window to your inner world, where you can observe with kindness and without any expectations.

So, my friend, the practice of mindfulness is like being that peaceful observer by the river of your mind. Embrace this beautiful state of presence and acceptance, and let it guide you to a calmer and more centered life.

Dr. Kabat-Zinn, a renowned mindfulness expert, said, "Attention is the faculty that allows us to navigate our lives in one way or another and to actually know what's happening or know that we don't know what's happening and find ways to be in a wiser relationship to things that are going on in our lives [rather] than being at the mercy, say, of our own emotional reactions and crazy thoughts and fears and so forth."

Her statement beautifully highlights how mindfulness becomes our superpower, empowering us to navigate life with wisdom and resilience. By honing this amazing ability to pay deliberate attention, we gain deep insights into our thoughts, emotions, and reactions.

No more getting swept away in the chaos of our minds or tossed around by external circumstances! With mindfulness, we're like skillful captains steering our ship, choosing how we respond to each moment that comes our way. It's like having a secret weapon that helps us find clarity and peace amidst life's ups and downs.

So, my friend, embrace this faculty of attention and embark on a journey of self-discovery and inner strength. With mindfulness by your side, you'll face each day with a heart full of resilience and a mind brimming with wisdom. You have the power to shape your own path, starting with being present and mindful.

When it comes to overthinking, mindfulness becomes our superhero, breaking the chains of relentless rumination. As we practice mindfulness, we become aware of those repetitive thought patterns that keep us in the worry loop. It's like shining a light on those negative clouds that affect our well-being.

With non-judgmental observation, we gain the power to detach ourselves from these thoughts. It's like stepping back and seeing them for what they are without getting tangled up in their grip. This act allows us to take charge of our minds once again. Mindfulness helps us detach from the past and future, grounding us in the here and now, where we can find solace, joy, and a renewed sense of clarity.

Embracing mindfulness is like opening the door to a transformative adventure! It's a journey that leads us to break free from the chains of overthinking and step into a world of liberation.

As we walk this path, we discover the power to nurture our mental well-being, like a gentle gardener tending to the blossoms of our minds. Mindfulness helps us find peace within, fostering a more fulfilling and meaningful life.

So, let's take that leap together, hand in hand, and embark on this beautiful journey toward liberation and self-discovery. With mindfulness as our guide, we'll uncover the magic within ourselves and embrace a life of serenity and joy. Trust the process, and watch as you blossom into your best self.

6 STRATEGIES TO STOP OVERTHINKING

In this section, we embark on a journey to the fortress of the quiet mind, unveiling six master keys to silence the whispers of overthinking:

1. The Awareness Diary

An awareness diary is like a special book where you can write down your thoughts and feelings. It's like having a personal journal where you can pour out your heart and put your emotions into words.

Imagine it as your trusted friend, always there to listen without judgment. Writing in this diary is like getting your thoughts out of your head and onto paper. It helps you see things more clearly, like turning on a light in a dark room.

It's a safe place to explore your feelings, understand yourself better, and let go of any worries or fears. Writing in your awareness diary can be like a calming escape, a way to express yourself and find peace.

So, give it a try! Grab a pen and let your thoughts flow onto the pages of your awareness diary. You might be surprised at how liberating and comforting it feels.

2. Sitting in Discomfort

Imagine overthinking as a wild beast born from our fear of discomfort and the unknown. Instead of running away, face it head-on. Embrace the pain it brings and feel its raw, untamed power without judgment.

It's like sitting beside this beast, observing it closely without fear. As we learn to coexist with it, the chains of overthinking slowly loosen their grip. We become more in control and less overwhelmed by its presence.

Be brave and face the wild beast of overthinking. Embrace the discomfort and watch as its power diminishes. With time and practice, you'll find a sense of calm and freedom, knowing that you can handle whatever thoughts come your way.

3. Embracing Uncertainty

Life's dance floor can sometimes feel like it's covered in uncertainty, making every step slippery. But instead of fighting against the unpredictable rhythm, let's embrace it with open arms. Overthinking is like trying to choreograph a perfect dance, but in reality, life's dance is beautifully imperfect.

So, my friend, let's release the need for absolute control and allow ourselves to dance freely with uncertainty. It's like a liberating waltz of acceptance and adaptability. Embrace the twists and turns, knowing it's okay not to have all the answers.

As we let go of the pressure to be perfect, we'll find joy in the dance of life. So, dance on, my friend, with courage and an open heart. Embrace the uncertainty and discover the beauty of living in the moment. You're a fantastic dancer in this grand ballroom of life!

4. Meditation

Meditation is a powerful practice for quieting the mind and cultivating present-moment awareness. Meditation is like a conductor of a silent symphony, directing the cacophony of your mind toward a harmonious silence. With every meditative breath, watch your thoughts flow like notes in a song without losing yourself in the melody. This is the dance of detachment, the calm within the storm of thoughts.

Embrace this serene practice and find your inner conductor, directing your mind towards harmony and stillness. It's a journey of self-discovery and peace.

5. The Four-Step Pause

Feeling caught up in the whirlwind of overthinking? Take a break and find solace in the four-step pause. It's like stepping into a cozy sanctuary with four corners where you can find peace.

First, take a deep breath to ground yourself. Then, without judging yourself, label the thoughts swirling in your mind. Release their hold on you, letting them pass like clouds in the sky. Finally, anchor yourself to the present moment by focusing on a simple sensation, like the feeling of your breath or the touch of your hand.

This sanctuary of the four-step pause is your safe harbor from the storm of overthinking. It's a gentle reminder to pause, breathe, and find calm amidst the chaos.

6. Engage in Mindful Activities

Mindful activities are like an elixir, soothing the gnawing itch of overthinking. Whether it's yoga, nature walks, or painting, these activities draw you into the rich tapestry of the present moment. As you immerse in the sensory experience, overthinking dissipates, replaced by a tranquil sense of flow.

Implement these keys into your daily routine and take charge of your overthinking. Remember, the journey to peace is a marathon, not a sprint, so take each step with patience and kindness toward yourself as you dethrone the tyranny of overthinking.

THE ROLE OF MINDFULNESS IN BUILDING TRUST AND INTIMACY

With its unique focus on being fully present and accepting without judgment, mindfulness becomes a beautiful foundation for trust and intimacy in relationships. When both partners practice mindfulness, they create a safe and loving space to truly hear, see, and understand each other.

Imagine it as a cozy cocoon of compassion and connection. With mindfulness, you become more attuned to each other's needs and feelings. It's like having a secret language that allows you to communicate with your heart.

So, let me guide you through some beautiful ways mindfulness enhances trust and intimacy. Together, we'll explore this magical practice and deepen the bond between you and your partner. It's a journey of love and growth, where every moment becomes a precious gift. Let's dive in and embrace the power of mindfulness in your beautiful relationship!

1. Deepening Communication

Imagine mindfulness as a magical loom, skillfully crafting intricate tapestries of genuine connection and deep understanding in your relationship. When you practice mindfulness, it's like threading together precious moments with your partner, creating a beautiful fabric of love and intimacy.

As you listen attentively to your partner's words, you're not just hearing echoes but genuinely absorbing their heartfelt whispers. This creates a special realm of communication where your partner feels cherished and seen, fostering a deep sense of trust and love.

Think of mindfulness as a trustworthy anchor that keeps your relationship steady and strong. It's like a nurturing force that weaves a lasting bond between you and your partner. With mindfulness, every interaction becomes an opportunity to strengthen your connection.

So, my dear reader, let's embrace this enchanted mindfulness practice together. Allow it to be the loom that weaves warmth, understanding, and love into your relationship's fabric. With each mindful moment, you'll see your connection grow stronger and more profound. Happy weaving, and may your tapestry of love be a masterpiece!

2. Developing Emotional Intelligence

Picture mindfulness as your wise and caring guide, walking hand-in-hand with you through the labyrinth of emotions in yourself and your partner. It's like having an emotional compass that helps you navigate the waves of feelings.

This heightened awareness opens the door to empathy's magical shores, where understanding and compassion thrive. And guess what? Empathy is the cornerstone of trust and intimacy in any relationship.

Knowing that, embrace mindfulness as your loving companion on this emotional journey. Take the time to explore the depths of your emotions, cultivating empathy and building a strong bond with your partner. It's a cozy and heartwarming adventure where every step brings you closer to a deeper connection and a more fulfilling relationship.

3. Cultivating Non-reactivity

Mindfulness in your relationship allows you to remain calm and composed when your partner expresses their thoughts and feelings. Instead of reacting impulsively, you respond with compassion and kindness, creating a safe and understanding environment for both of you. This builds trust and strengthens your bond.

Imagine mindfulness as a tool that helps you navigate emotional situations with grace and empathy. It's like a secret ingredient that enhances your ability to listen and be present for your partner. This mindful approach nurtures a loving atmosphere where both of you feel valued and acknowledged.

Practicing mindfulness can foster a deeper connection and create a loving space where trust can flourish. It's a journey of growth and understanding where both partners can support and uplift each other. Together, you'll make your relationship a harmonious and loving place to be.

4. Nurturing Vulnerability

Mindfulness is a gentle invitation to a sacred dance with vulnerability, where both partners shed their armor to share their deepest thoughts and fears. Unshielded from judgment or rejection, this naked truth forms the crucible where emotional connection deepens and intimacy thrives.

Let's consider a practical example to illustrate the power of mindfulness and vulnerability in a relationship:

Imagine Sarah and Alex, a couple who have been together for a few years. Recently, Sarah has been feeling overwhelmed by work stress and struggling with self-confidence. In the past, she would have bottled up her

156 | S.G. FONTES

emotions and put on a brave face, not wanting to burden Alex with her worries.

However, with mindfulness practice, Sarah learns to embrace vulnerability and share her feelings with Alex. One evening, as they sit down to talk, Sarah takes a deep breath and opens up about her struggles and fears. Instead of judging or trying to fix the problem, Alex listens attentively and responds with empathy and kindness.

In this moment of vulnerability and honest sharing, their emotional connection deepens. Sarah feels seen, heard, and supported, and Alex feels closer to her than ever. Through mindfulness and vulnerability, they create a safe space where both partners can be authentic to themselves.

As they continue to practice mindfulness and vulnerability in their relationship, they find that their bond grows stronger, and their intimacy flourishes. They become each other's support pillars, navigating life's challenges with love and understanding.

This practical example shows how mindfulness and vulnerability can transform relationships, nurturing a deeper emotional connection and fostering a loving and supportive environment. By being open and honest with each other, Sarah and Alex create a relationship where trust and intimacy thrive.

5. Enhancing Intimacy

Think of mindfulness practices as magical alchemy, turning ordinary moments into golden memories of intimate connection. For instance, try a mindful touch moment with your partner. Hold hands or give each other a gentle back rub, focusing on the sensation and the love you share. You'll transform a fleeting instant into a precious and lasting bond between you both in that simple act. It's like weaving threads of closeness that will bind your hearts together, creating a beautiful tapestry of love and intimacy in your relationship.

MINDFULNESS PRACTICES FOR COUPLES: 5 WAYS TO SHOW YOUR PARTNER YOU CARE — JUST BY BEING MINDFUL

Confining mindfulness to yourself is not always enough. You will also need to encircle your relationship in the realm of care and mindfulness. So, let's look at a few ways to make your partner feel loved.

1. Take a breath

Before responding to your partner, take a conscious breath to ground yourself in the present moment (Lehal, 2018). This pause lets you respond with clarity and kindness, promoting understanding and reducing conflict.

2. Give a compliment

Notice and acknowledge your partner's positive qualities or efforts. Express sincere appreciation for them. A mindful compliment can uplift their spirits and strengthen the bond between them.

3. Silence their critic

When your partner expresses vulnerability or shares a concern, be fully present and non-judgmental. Offer support and reassurance, creating a safe space for them to be authentic and validated.

4. Avoid triggers

Mindfully observe your triggers and reactions that may cause tension or conflict in the relationship. Choose to respond rather than react impulsively, allowing for open and constructive dialogue.

5. Invite them

Encourage your partner to join you in mindfulness practices such as meditation, yoga, or nature walks (Lehal, 2018). Sharing these experiences fosters a deeper connection and a mutual commitment to growth and well-being.

Remember, building trust and intimacy takes time and effort. Incorporating mindfulness into your relationship creates a foundation of love, understanding, and empathy. Approach each moment with genuine presence and compassion, and watch as your bond deepens and flourishes.

MINDFULNESS PRACTICAL EXERCISES AND TIPS

Harnessing the power of mindfulness is like growing a garden - it calls for consistent nurturing, tender care, and, above all, patience. Let's embark on a journey to unearth some exercises and tips that could serve as your gardening tools to cultivate the seeds of mindfulness.

1. **Mindful Eating**: Transform your mealtime into a banquet of mindful discovery. Attend the kaleidoscope of colors, the tapestry of textures, and the symphony of flavors of your food. Slow your pace, savor each morsel, letting the tastes dance on your tongue. Immerse entirely in the moment, free of distractions, and cultivate a moment of gratitude for the nourishment your meal offers.
2. **Mindful Walking**: Extract yourself from the whirlwind of daily life and embark on a mindful walk. As you do that, tune in to the gentle kiss of the earth beneath your feet, the rhythmic sway of

your body, and the world blooming around you. Ignite your senses, observing the landscape of sights, sounds, and scents enveloping you. Allow your mind to actively participate in the act of walking, savoring the poetry of each step.

3. **Body Scan**: Carve out a quiet moment each day for a body mapping practice. Settle into a comfortable position, sitting or lying down, and usher your attention on a voyage across your body. Start at your toes and sail upwards, noticing the whispers of sensations or the echoes of tension. Welcome these sensations without judgment and exhale any stress away. This practice is like a lullaby for the body, promoting relaxation and body awareness.

4. **Mindful Coloring**: Indulge in the tranquil art of mindful coloring. Choose a coloring book or print out a mindful coloring page. As you color, focus on the strokes of your pencil or crayon. The colors emerging on the page and the rhythmic movements of your hand. Allow yourself to immerse fully in the process, letting go of thoughts or worries. Coloring can be a calming and creative practice.

5. **Mindful Meditation**: Dedicate a quiet interlude each day for a formal mindfulness meditation practice. Locate a tranquil space where interruptions can't find you. Settle comfortably and draw your attention to your breath, using it to

anchor your focus. As thoughts arise, gently acknowledge them without judgment and bring your attention back to your breath. Cultivate an attitude of curiosity and kindness towards your experience. Start with shorter sessions and gradually increase the duration as you feel more comfortable.

Tips for Maximizing Mindfulness Practice

1. Ignite your senses, immersing them in the world's symphony of sights, sounds, aromas, tastes, and textures. Consider, for instance, the simple act of showering. Savor the sensation of water, a gentle waterfall, drumming on your skin, each droplet an individual caress, an invitation to be present.

2. Your mind will naturally veer off course like a feather in the wind. Observe its flight path, and witness where your thoughts take shelter. It can be beneficial to name these thoughts and emotions, a gentle whisper to yourself acknowledging their presence, such as, "Anger is visiting me now," or "There's that old companion, self-doubt."

3. Breathe in the intricate tapestry of emotions and sensations unfurling within your body. Instead of trying to extinguish or muzzle these feelings or thoughts, adopt the stance of a welcoming host,

meeting them with a curious smile absent of judgment.

4. Like a compass pointing north, consciously pivot your attention back to the present moment. This can be achieved by riding the ebb and flow of your breath or tuning into a physical sensation within your body. Or, you might shift your focus to the world around you, savoring each sensory detail, from the smell of rain-soaked earth to the distant song of a bird.

5. Remember, mindfulness is akin to taming a wild stallion, requiring patience, consistency, and compassion. When your mind wanders off, refrain from casting stones of criticism. Instead, like a shepherd guiding a lost lamb back to the flock, gently steer your attention to your mindfulness exercise, armed with kindness and understanding.

You open the door to a deeper connection with the present moment by weaving these powerful strategies into your mindfulness practice. Embrace the opportunity to be fully aware and compassionate with your thoughts and experiences, creating a beautiful garden of self-discovery and growth. With each step, you'll blossom into a more mindful and content version of yourself, savoring the richness of life's tapestry.

Practical Suggestions for Mindfulness

As we turn the last pages of this chapter, let me leave you with a trove of practical wisdom. The key to mastering mindfulness is like a steady heartbeat—consistent and rhythmical. Dedicate specific periods to immerse yourself in the tranquility of mindfulness.

Think of short, frequent sessions as tiny nourishing droplets that often hydrate your mindfulness plant better than sporadic downpours. Time constraints should not be barriers but bridges—transform mundane tasks like washing dishes or showering into mindful moments.

Craft a sanctuary, a peaceful haven free from the clamor of distractions, where you can sink into mindfulness. This may be a cozy corner indoors or an open expanse under the sky's infinite canvas—wherever your spirit finds peace.

See mindfulness as a journey, not a destination. Instead of sprinting, take leisurely strides, slowly increasing your mindfulness stamina without imposing pressure. Remember, you're cultivating a skill; growth is an evolving process.

Discard the map of "right" and "wrong." Let go of the quest for perfection and rigid adherence. Paint your mindfulness practice with strokes of personal adaptation. Remember, comfort in the course often comes with time, like a new pair of shoes slowly molding to the shape of your feet.

Remember, mindfulness is an intimate dance with yourself, choreographed to your unique rhythm. Savor the privilege of this journey at your own pace, enriching your daily life with mindful moments and experiencing the myriad benefits it brings.

This chapter invites you to discover the transformative power of mindfulness to liberate us from the chains of overthinking and to guide us toward an awakened existence. We have meandered through a garden of mindful eating, walking, and meditation techniques that help us foster deeper connections with ourselves and the world.

By weaving these practices into the fabric of our lives, we can shed layers of stress and discover a serene sanctuary within. The coming chapter will illuminate the path of gratitude. This potent force can recalibrate our perspectives, inviting us to see life's blessings hidden in plain sight.

We will sow gratitude in our individual lives and relationships with practical strategies and exercises. A thankful heart springs to boundless joy, contentment, and fulfillment.

So, let's journey together into the landscape of gratitude, exploring its profound influence on our well-being and relationships. Brace yourself to unearth tangible ways to nurture appreciation and embrace life's abundance.

8

CULTIVATING GRATITUDE AND APPRECIATION

Wanting perfection in our relationships and personal lives is a dilemma that each of us crosses simultaneously. After all, wouldn't the world be a perfect place if everyone did as they pleased in a relationship? But then, what would the repercussions be?

After all, sometimes, our minds can't help but wander and wonder about how we can spice things up in our relationships. It's pretty natural to think about the "what ifs" or the "what could have been." But guess what? Instead of dwelling on the gaps, why not focus on the gold? Yep, I'm hinting at embracing gratitude and cherishing the good moments.

In this chapter, let's dive into some fun and simple ways to boost our gratitude game. I'll share the charm of jotting down your thankful moments in a gratitude journal and the calming beauty of mindfulness. Think of these as your feel-good toolkit, ready to sprinkle positivity when those overthinking clouds loom.

With regular expressions of gratitude and appreciation, you can create a relationship that's not just strong but also joyous and fulfilling. Are you ready to turn the page and start this enriching journey toward cultivating gratitude and appreciation in your relationship? Let's dive in!

THE ROLE OF GRATITUDE AND APPRECIATION IN REDUCING OVERTHINKING

Gratitude is a warm feeling of thankfulness towards the world or towards specific individuals. It's like a personal spotlight that you can shine on the things you appreciate, helping you notice and enjoy them more (Psychology Today, 2019). When we practice gratitude, we're not ignoring life's hardships but choosing to focus on what's going well.

It works like a mental muscle – the more you use it, the stronger it gets. Studies show that regularly practicing gratitude can lead to feeling more positive emotions, improving our health, and even building stronger relationships (Psychology Today, 2019). In a nutshell, gratitude can be a key ingredient for a happier, healthier you.

5 MENTAL HEALTH BENEFITS OF GRATITUDE

In learning about gratitude and practicing it in a relationship, it is important to remember that it, first and foremost, helps you. After all, a healthier you, with a pretty mindset, can help transform your relationship. So, now let us take a look at some of the mental health benefits associated with gratitude.

1. **Gratitude Can Help Regulate Your Emotions**: Adopting a gratitude practice can act as an emotional thermostat. Have you ever heard of an emotional thermostat? That's what gratitude can be for us (McDermott & Spann, 2022). When we take a moment to soak in what we're thankful for, it keeps our emotional boat steady, making the rough seas of life a tad easier to navigate.

2. **Gratitude Can Elevate Your Mindset**: Gratitude has the power to shift your perspective. By focusing on things you appreciate, you condition your mind to lean more toward positivity (McDermott & Spann, 2022). It's like having your very own mindset elevator. By cherishing the good stuff, you're gently nudging your thoughts towards sunny skies. The result? A brighter outlook and a bounce in your step.

3. **Gratitude Can Reduce Stress**: Stress can get the best of us, but gratitude can help. When we count our blessings, those big worries start looking

much smaller, and that chaotic mind? It gets a chill pill.

4. **Gratitude Can Improve Self-esteem:** Here's a fun side effect of being thankful – you start to see the awesomeness in you, too! When we're feeling grateful, it spills over, letting us see our achievements and the little victories, making us go, "Hey, I'm pretty amazing!"

5. **Gratitude Can Promote Better Sleep:** Grateful thoughts can replace worry and the mental to-do lists that often keep us awake (McDermott & Spann, 2022). After all, those pesky nighttime worries and endless to-do lists? They're no match for gratitude. We're paving the way for some dreamy, restful slumber by ending the day with a dose of thankfulness.

HOW TO MAKE GRATITUDE PART OF YOUR DAILY PRACTICE: PRACTICAL IDEAS

Isn't it intriguing how the simple act of practicing gratitude can enhance our mental well-being and overall joy? Yes, it's true! When we direct our attention towards the blessings in our lives and nurture a feeling of thankfulness, we can feel more positive, mitigate stress, and potentially boost our physical health.

If you are eager to start your journey towards gratitude, then here are a few straightforward tips to help you kickstart:

Maintain a gratitude journal: Note three things that brought you joy each night. From relishing a delicious cup of coffee to spending time with a cherished friend or relative, when you spotlight the positives, you begin to grow your sense of happiness and thankfulness. (Look out for a Gratitude template at this chapter's conclusion).

Engage in gratitude meditation: Daily, allocate a few peaceful moments to ponder aspects you're thankful for. Envision a situation or person that evokes gratitude and let those feelings sink in.

Express your thanks: Make it a habit to show your thankfulness to people around you. A simple "thank you" to the person who brewed your coffee or a heartfelt message to a supportive friend can go a long way.

Bookending your day with gratitude: Start your day on a grateful note by thinking of something you're thankful for, even before stepping out of bed. Similarly, end your day by reflecting on the positive aspects, promoting a happier outlook.

Initiate a gratitude jar: Grab a jar and some notepapers. Each day, jot down one grateful aspect and place it in the jar. Over time, you'll accumulate a treasure of grateful moments you can revisit for an instant uplift.

Reorient Your Language, Transform Your Mindset: The words you use play a significant role in shaping your reality. By replacing negative language with positive, you can drastically shift your mindset and foster a deep sense of gratitude.

Schedule dedicated gratitude practice time: Regularly setting aside time for gratitude practices encourages consistent cultivation of thankfulness. It could be a specific time each day or a special weekly moment.

Share with others about your gratitude journey: Talking about your experiences with gratitude can inspire others and enhance your own practice. Sharing your journey can make it more meaningful and rewarding.

Picture your joyful instances: Mentally revisiting moments of joy and thankfulness can uplift your mood instantly. This practice enhances the feeling of gratitude, which positively impacts your overall well-being.

Curtail the negative self-talk: Paying attention to how you talk to yourself is crucial. When you stop criticizing yourself and replace it with kind, appreciative words, you make room for gratitude and positivity.

Embark on a gratitude stroll: A simple walk, where you observe and appreciate your surroundings, can help cultivate gratitude. Every tree, bird, or even the sound of leaves under your feet can remind you of life's gifts.

Smile more: A smile is a simple and effective way to express gratitude. Not only does it brighten up your mood, but it also spreads positivity to those around you. A cheerful demeanor can be a powerful gratitude practice.

Remember, by making gratitude a part of your daily practice, you will shift your focus from the negative aspects of life to the positive. This can have a profound impact on your mental health and overall happiness.

"Overcome Your Overthinking" The Benefits of Gratitude Practice

Now that we have looked at gratitude's crucial role, let's talk about why gratitude is the secret sauce to getting out of our heads and into our hearts.

We all know that taking the time to ponder decisions is super valuable. But when our minds get all buzzy with worry and start overanalyzing every tiny detail, we dive deep into the pool of overthinking. And trust me, that's not a fun place to be.

Overthinking not only stresses us out but also messes with our creativity, takes up way too much of our time, and doesn't even help us solve problems. It's like getting stuck in a mental loop, right?

That's where gratitude slides in. According to Dr. Heidi Sormaz, who's like this yoga genius from Fresh Yoga LLC, gratitude isn't just saying "thanks." In her fantastic video series, 'Overcome Your Overthinking,' She chats about how gratitude is about genuinely feeling that warm and fuzzy appreciation for the good stuff in our lives.

Here's a cool nugget from Dr. Sormaz: when we tap into gratitude, it's like giving our happiness a significant boost! Not only that, it's great for our health and can be a game-changer for those dealing with mental health challenges. In her own words, "When we're filled with gratitude, it's like our bodies, moods, and thoughts all get a positive jolt. Plus, it makes us more open-minded, helping us see tricky situations in a new light" (Writer, 2022).

Dr. Sormaz also highlights that being grateful can super-charge our brain with happy chemicals like serotonin and dopamine. These are like the brain's feel-good buddies that shoo away anxiety and those down-in-the-dump feelings. Even cooler? Gratitude can give our brain a little tune-up, especially the part that handles those not-so-fun emotions.

And if that wasn't enough, thanking your lucky stars can also score you some bonus sleep points. When we dive into gratitude, our brain's sleep manager, the hypothalamus, is all geared up. Studies have even shown that with more gratitude comes better sleep – both in quality and how long we're off in dreamland.

So, next time you find yourself caught in a whirlwind of thoughts, remember to pause and count your blessings. Your mind, body, and sleep schedule will thank you!

STRATEGIES TO EXPRESS GRATITUDE AND APPRECIATION TO YOUR PARTNER

Now that we know that overthinking can be avoided by expressing gratitude, it is time to focus on ways to show gratitude and appreciation for your partner.

1. **Notice the little things**: Be mindful of the small, everyday gestures your partner does for you. It could be as simple as them making you a cup of coffee in the morning or giving you a warm smile after a long day. Expressing gratitude for these moments can make your partner feel loved and appreciated.

2. **Talk in your partner's love language:** Dr. Gary Chapman identified five ways that people tend to express and experience love: Words of affirmation, gifts, quality time, acts of service, and physical touch (Mueller, 2018). Knowing your partner's love language can help you show gratitude in a way that deeply resonates with them. For example, if their love language is an act of service, doing the dishes or cooking dinner might be a powerful way to express gratitude.

3. **Give them your full attention**: In the age of smartphones and endless distractions, giving your undivided attention can be a significant form of gratitude. By putting away your device and actively listening to your partner, you can show

that you value their presence and what they have to say.

4. **Remember important dates**: Remembering and celebrating essential dates like anniversaries or birthdays shows your partner you care. It's not about the grandeur of the celebration but the thought and effort you put into making the day memorable for them.

5. **Compliment them in private & public**: Complimenting your partner in private is excellent, but doing so in front of others adds a layer of sincerity (Capanna-Hodge, 2021). It could be complimenting their dressing style at a party or acknowledging their hard work at a family gathering.

6. **Get creative with your gratitude:** Write a heartfelt note, create a surprise video montage of your shared memories, or even write a song to express your gratitude. The uniqueness of your expression adds more weight to your words of thanks.

7. **Acknowledge the things you'd usually take for granted:** Saying a genuine thank you for things you typically overlook, like them filling up your car's fuel tank or ensuring there's always milk in the fridge, can go a long way in expressing your gratitude.

8. **Support your partner's passions and dreams:** Show your gratitude by supporting their

aspirations, whether attending their amateur guitar gig or helping them set up their home garden. This shows you value their happiness and are grateful for their presence in your life.

9. **Make your partner feel important:** Encourage them when they are unsure, comfort them when they are down, and celebrate their achievements. These gestures of gratitude make them feel valued and important.

10. **Make gratitude a habit**: Make it a daily ritual to express gratitude to your partner. It could be sharing one thing you're thankful for over dinner or writing it on a sticky note for them to find. This constant appreciation cycle can enhance the bond you share with your partner.

By weaving these strategies into your love story, you're on your way to crafting a rock-solid and healthy relationship foundation. But before we move on, let's chat about another nifty trick to dodge that pesky overthinking habit. Ready? Let's go!

Gratitude Journal

So far, I have mentioned a gratitude journal many times but not in depth. Now, let us walk through what exactly a gratitude journal is. Well, a gratitude journal is a tool designed to help you cultivate a habit of recognizing and expressing thanks for the good aspects of life. It's a special notebook where you record daily entries of moments, people, or things that brought you joy, peace, or comfort, thus amplifying positive feelings.

But how exactly does a gratitude journal improve your well-being and relationship? Well, let's take a look!

Improve the quality of your sleep

Have you ever had trouble falling asleep because your mind won't stop racing? It can be so frustrating! When you take the time to reflect on the things you're grateful for

before bedtime, it can help to promote relaxation and calmness.

Instead of worrying about everything that went wrong during the day, you can focus on your life's positive experiences and blessings. This can help shift your mindset away from negative thoughts and worries that can keep you awake and promote feelings of peace and contentment that can lead to a better night's sleep.

But it's not just about what you write in your journal - it's also about the act of journaling itself. Taking a few minutes each night to sit down and reflect on your day can be a grounding and soothing experience. By putting your thoughts and feelings down on paper, you can release any pent-up emotions or worries that may keep you up at night.

So, if you're struggling with getting a good night's sleep, give gratitude journaling a try! You might be surprised at how much it can help you feel more relaxed, content, and ready to drift off into dreamland.

Reduce stress

Keeping a journal is a powerful tool for reducing stress and overthinking in relationships. When we're in a romantic partnership, it's easy to get caught up in our thoughts and worries, especially when things aren't going as smoothly as we'd like.

That's where a gratitude journal can come in handy!

Taking the time to write down the things you're grateful for in your relationship can help shift your focus away from any negative feelings or concerns you may be dwelling on.

Maybe you're grateful for your partner's sense of humor, or the way they always know how to cheer you up when you're feeling down. By reflecting on these positive aspects of your relationship, you can cultivate a sense of appreciation and contentment that can help to reduce stress and anxiety.

Additionally, journaling can be a helpful way to process and release any negative emotions that you may be experiencing. Maybe you're feeling frustrated or hurt by something your partner said or did. Writing about these feelings in your journal can be a therapeutic and cathartic experience, providing a safe space to express yourself and work through any difficult emotions.

Overall, keeping a gratitude journal can be a powerful way to promote positivity, reduce stress, and cultivate a more balanced and resilient mindset in your relationship. Give it a try and see how it can help you feel more grounded, connected, and grateful for the special person in your life.

Increase positivity

A gratitude journal can be a powerful way to increase positivity in your life and relationships. It's all about focusing on the good things!

Taking the time to write down the things you're grateful for each day can help shift your mindset toward positivity. Maybe you're thankful for the beautiful weather, a delicious meal, or the support of a loved one (Capanna-Hodge, 2021). By reflecting on these positive experiences and blessings in your life, you can cultivate a sense of appreciation and joy that can help to counteract any negative thoughts or feelings you may be experiencing.

And when it comes to relationships, gratitude journaling can be especially powerful. Reflecting on the things we appreciate about our partners can help us feel more connected and loving towards them.

Maybe you're grateful for your partner's sense of humor, kindness, or how they always listen to you. By reflecting on these positive qualities and experiences, you can strengthen your bond with your partner and foster a more positive and loving dynamic in your relationship.

Overall, keeping a gratitude journal can be a simple yet powerful way to increase positivity and joy in your life and your relationships.

Strengthen self-worth

Keeping a journal can be a wonderful tool for strengthening your self-worth, which can hugely positively impact your relationship. When you take the time to reflect on your accomplishments, your strengths, and the things you're proud of, it can help boost your confidence and sense of self-worth.

Maybe you're proud of a project you completed at work, a new skill you've learned, or a personal challenge you've overcome. By writing about these achievements and reflecting on how they make you feel, you can cultivate a greater sense of self-esteem and self-respect.

And when it comes to relationships, having a strong sense of self-worth can be incredibly beneficial. Feeling good about ourselves and our abilities can help us communicate more clearly, set healthy boundaries, and engage in relationships from a place of strength rather than insecurity. By valuing and respecting ourselves, we're more likely to attract partners who do the same and engage in fulfilling and positive relationships.

Take some time each day to reflect on your achievements, strengths, and what you're proud of. By cultivating a greater sense of self-worth, you'll be better equipped to navigate your relationships from a place of strength and positivity.

Help you celebrate the present

Keeping a journal can be a wonderful way to celebrate the present moment and all its beauty and joy. By reflecting on the things we're grateful for and the positive experiences we've had each day, we can cultivate a greater sense of appreciation and mindfulness for the present moment.

Maybe you had a great conversation with a friend, enjoyed a delicious cup of coffee, or felt a sense of peace and contentment in your surroundings. By reflecting on these moments and savoring the joy they bring, we can celebrate the present and all the goodness it offers.

And celebrating the present moment can be especially beneficial when it comes to relationships. When fully present and engaged, we can better connect with our partners and enjoy our time together.

Whether going for a walk, cooking a meal together, or simply snuggling up on the couch, taking the time to be present and enjoy these moments can help us deepen our connections with our partners and foster a greater sense of appreciation and love.

As the famous writer and theologian Meister Eckhart once said, "If the only prayer you ever say in your entire life is "thank you", it will be enough." By celebrating the present and all the blessings it has to offer, we can cultivate a greater sense of gratitude, joy, and love in our lives and relationships. So take a moment each day to reflect on the good things in your life and savor the beauty and joy of the present moment.

Possibly lower the risk of heart disease

Keeping a journal can be a great way to care for yourself and your relationships! When we're feeling stressed or anxious, it can take a toll on our health and our ability to connect with others. But by regularly reflecting on positive experiences and cultivating a sense of gratitude and positivity, journaling can help to reduce stress and promote emotional well-being.

Research suggests that practicing gratitude journaling can even lower the risk of heart disease! By reducing stress hormones like cortisol, journaling can have a positive impact on our physical health as well as our emotional well-being.

And the best part? Taking care of yourself can also benefit your relationships! We're more present, compassionate, and loving partners when we feel good. So, if you're looking to improve your health and relationships, consider starting a journal.

Take time each day to reflect on the good things in your life and see how they can make a difference in your overall well-being and connections with loved ones.

To help you get started, I have picked 30 of my favorite prompts to help me write in my gratitude journal (Kristenson, 2022). You can also choose your favorite from these and let the words flow.

1. Jot down a recent moment that gave you those feel-good vibes.
2. Think of people you think are just awesome. What traits do they have that you want more of in your life?
3. What are five things that instantly bring a grin to your face? Why's that?
4. List five pieces of nature's beauty that you cherish.
5. Brainstorm three kind of acts you can do this week, and make it happen!
6. What particular thing about your job or workplace buddies that brightens your day?
7. Got any cool ideas to spruce up your neighborhood?
8. What do you totally love about where you live?
9. Dive deep into what makes your all-time favorite person so great.
10. Dream up four little things that could bring someone joy, and sprinkle that joy around this week.

11. Have you ever paused to really cherish your senses? Reflect on that.

12. What (or who) turns your house into a home?

13. Think of three tough times you crushed. How did they shape the awesome person you are today?

14. Give yourself a high-five and list three things you genuinely like about yourself.

15. Got a go-to comfort food? Why's it special?

16. Ponder ways to sprinkle more thank-you moments into your everyday.

17. Recall something that made you laugh till you cried.

18. How can you lend a hand to someone who might need a boost?

19. Dive into the unique vibes your pals bring into your life.

20. That song that tugs at your heartstrings - why's it got you hooked?

21. List 10 of your trusty gadgets or gizmos that simplify life.

22. Facing a hurdle? Sketch out a baby step to start tackling it.

23. Got a neighbor? Think of a tiny gesture to make their day shine.

24. Know someone who grates on you? Challenge: find one thing to appreciate about them!

25. Is there an artwork that "gets" you? Dive into why.

26. Got a pet peeve? Spin it! How can you find a silver lining in it?

27. Describe a scent that's... chef's kiss. What memories does it stir?
28. Which book is your safety blanket? Why's it your repeat-read?
29. Give a shout-out to an educator who made a mark on you. What's their magic?
30. Have you ever goofed up and learned a golden lesson? Write about that wisdom!

At the end of the day, remember these are just jumping-off points. What will make your gratitude journal truly special are your own experiences and reflections. Remember to enjoy the process.

How to Start a Gratitude Journal

After looking at the prompts, why not get into it? I have a fun thought! How about you start journaling by jotting down things you're grateful for each day? You can choose how many you want to list, but it's a good practice to get into. The key here, my friend, is consistency.

1. Start by listing everyday items or things you're happy to own.
2. Dive deeper and think about personal traits or skills you're proud to possess.
3. Remember to shout out to the awesome folks in your life who light up your days.

4. And, of course, reminisce about uplifting moments or events that left a mark. This practice is sure to keep gratitude at the forefront!

HOW TO START A GRATITUDE JOURNAL (SAMPLE OF DAILY GRATITUDE JOURNAL)

Gratitude Journal:

Date:

_____

Today, I am thankful for:

1.

_____

_____

2.

_____

_____

3.

_____

188 | S.G. FONTES

Remember, gratitude journaling is something you can personalize to make it work for you. The important thing is to create a habit of reflecting on the good things in your life and cultivating a thankful attitude. So, feel free to make it your own and keep up with it regularly!

Example:

Date: October 23, 2023

Today, I am thankful for:

1- The sunrise this morning painted the sky with hues of orange and pink.

2- A colleague's supportive and encouraging words helped boost my confidence at work.

3- Celebrating my love's birthday with him.

4. What brought joy to my day?

_____

_____

5. What was one small victory that made me proud?

_____

_____

6. What lesson did I learn today?

_____

_____

7. In what ways did today surpass my expectations?

_____

_____

8. I could complete a difficult task at work that I had been struggling with for a while, which gave me a sense of accomplishment.

_____

_____

9. How did I take care of myself today?

_____

_____

Remember, the purpose of this journal is to focus on the positives in your life and develop a mindset of gratitude.

Take time each day to reflect on your answers and appreciate the good things in your life, no matter how small they may seem.

Also, here is a Gratitude Journal sample, focused on your partner with daily questions to answer:

Date:

_____

What is one thing my partner did today that I'm grateful for?

_____

_____

Why am I grateful for this?

_____

_____

What is one quality about my partner that I appreciate?

_____

_____

What is one positive memory I have with my partner?

_____

_____

What is one thing I can do to show my partner how much I

appreciate them?

_____

_____

How does my partner make my life better?

_____

_____

What is one way I can support my partner today?

_____

_____

Hey, the point of this journal is to show your partner how much you appreciate them and strengthen your relationship. So, take a little time each day to reflect on your answers and let your partner know how grateful you are for them. It's not just about saying it; try to show them how much you care through your actions, too.

Let's use this gratitude journal to make our bond even stronger! Do you know what makes a relationship awesome? Gratitude and appreciation! When we take a minute to notice and appreciate the good stuff in our partner, it makes our bond super strong.

No challenge can get in the way of that. When we're thankful for the little and big things, we start to feel happier and more fulfilled in our relationship. So let's not take our loved ones for granted, and always ensure they know how much we appreciate them!

To summarize things, in this chapter, we delved into the transformative power of gratitude within romantic relationships. The essence of our discussion revolved around how adopting an attitude of thankfulness can be a pivotal tool against the pitfalls of overthinking.

Through practical strategies like maintaining a gratitude journal and embracing mindfulness, we discovered avenues to magnify the positive aspects of our bond. But the journey doesn't end here.

Now, what do you need to do? Well, begin today by expressing a simple word of appreciation to your partner.

Whether it's a spoken word or a kind gesture, let gratitude be the compass that guides your relationship to deeper connection and fulfillment. Let's cherish every moment and make gratitude an integral part of our love story.

9

SELF-IMPROVEMENT TIPS TO UP YOUR GAME

Now that we are taking another step towards improvement, let's have a heart-to-heart moment. Do you know how we often talk about evolving and becoming the best versions of ourselves? This journey doesn't pause just because we're in a relationship. In fact, it becomes even more crucial.

Imagine a plant. It requires sunlight, water, and suitable soil to bloom fully. Similarly, our personal growth is like that plant, needing constant care and attention, even when deeply intertwined with someone else. Self-improvement isn't just about picking up a new hobby or hitting the gym (although, kudos to you if you're doing that!). It's about introspection and understanding our values, strengths, and areas that could use a bit of refining.

But why is self-improvement in a relationship so important? By understanding ourselves better, we become more articulate about our needs, desires, and boundaries. More transparent communication is like the secret sauce that makes relationships much smoother. In this chapter, I will walk you through some game-changing self-improvement tips.

THE BENEFITS OF PERSONAL GROWTH IN RELATIONSHIPS

While personal growth is a term we are all familiar with, it is crucial to take a slightly deeper look into what it means. At its core, personal growth refers to the continuous process of self-improvement and self-discovery (Lori Jean Glass, 2022). It's the dedication to understanding oneself better, expanding horizons, and acquiring skills and knowledge to lead a fulfilled life.

It's a lifelong quest that enables us to live up to our full potential, like leveling up in a video game. It's all about self-enhancement and evolving, but with a twist—it's like taking those tricky traits of ours and turning them into superpowers. And guess what? While you're still you, you become a shinier, more energized version of yourself!

Now, let's dive into the incredible benefits of personal growth in relationships, shall we?

1. Enhanced Communication Skills

Personal growth often involves developing better communication. By understanding ourselves more, we're more articulate in expressing our thoughts and feelings. This leads to deeper, more meaningful conversations with our partner, strengthening the bond.

2. Increased Emotional Intelligence

Emotional intelligence is like a sixth sense in relationships! Personal growth helps in recognizing not only our emotions but our partner's as well (Lori Jean Glass, 2022). It enables us to respond with empathy and kindness, fostering a loving and compassionate relationship.

3. Building Trust and Confidence

By working on ourselves, we instill confidence and trust within the relationship. Trust isn't just about being reliable; it's about believing in ourselves and our partner. This foundation of trust acts as a stronghold, making the relationship resilient.

4. Boosting Financial Harmony

Personal growth often includes financial awareness and responsibility. It's about aligning financial goals and working together towards them, creating a stress-free financial environment, and adding a unique layer of harmony to the relationship (Lori Jean Glass, 2022).

5. Fostering Spiritual Connection

Spiritual growth allows us to connect on a profound level. Whether sharing beliefs or engaging in spiritual practices together, it creates a soulful connection that transcends the mundane, adding a special spark to the relationship.

6. Improving Physical Well-being Together

Lastly, personal growth includes physical care. It's not just about hitting the gym; it's about embracing healthy habits together. Whether it's cooking a nutritious meal or going for a run, these shared activities promote a sense of teamwork and mutual encouragement.

Remember, personal growth is a multifaceted jewel in relationships. It's not just about being a better "me" but cultivating a thriving "us." So, take the plunge into personal growth and watch how it transforms not just you but your relationship into something truly extraordinary.

WHAT ARE THE KEY AREAS OF PERSONAL GROWTH?

The journey of personal growth is intricate and multifaceted, much like a mosaic where each tile contributes to a larger, beautiful picture. Each growth area provides unique challenges and rewards (Lori Jean Glass, 2022). Let's traverse through the five essential domains of personal growth:

1. Intellectual Growth

Intellectual growth is the cultivation of the mind. It's about seeking knowledge, honing critical thinking skills, and cultivating creativity (Lori Jean Glass, 2022). In a world constantly evolving, our intellectual capabilities help us remain relevant, adaptive, and innovative. Reading, debating, solving puzzles, or playing musical instruments contribute to intellectual expansion. This area ensures we always continue learning and exploring.

2. Financial Growth

Financial growth isn't merely about amassing wealth; it's about understanding the value of money, effective management, and making informed financial decisions. Whether budgeting, investing, or understanding the nuances of debt, financial growth ensures stability and paves the path for future aspirations. It teaches us the equilibrium between earning, saving, investing, and spending.

3. Spiritual Growth

Spiritual growth delves deep into our beliefs, values, and understanding of the universe and our place within it (Lori Jean Glass, 2022). Regardless of religious beliefs, this growth encompasses a deeper connection with oneself, nature, or a higher power. Meditation, reflection, and even acts of kindness can nurture the soul, bringing inner peace and a clearer understanding of life's purpose.

4. Emotional Growth

Emotional growth is the compass that guides our reactions and interactions. It's the development of emotional intelligence, which includes understanding, expressing, and managing our emotions. By improving our emotional well-being, we can forge stronger relationships, manage stress effectively, and navigate life's ups and downs with resilience.

5. Physical Growth

Our bodies are miraculous machines, and physical growth ensures we maintain and celebrate them. Whether through exercise, proper nutrition, or understanding the importance of rest, this domain is about respecting our physiological needs. A healthy body often leads to a healthy mind, completing the holistic growth cycle.

In the grand tapestry of life, each of these domains interweaves to form the person we become. Prioritizing growth in these areas ensures a balanced, enriched life and equips us with tools to craft our best selves.

HOW TO ACHIEVE PERSONAL GROWTH

Now that we have talked so much about personal growth, it's important to consider how you can achieve it. Here are my top picks, and you can also pick your favorites.

1. **Dive into Books:** Reading regularly, both fiction and nonfiction, expands the mind. Fiction transports us to different worlds, cultivating empathy, while nonfiction augments our

knowledge, keeping us informed and enlightened (Lori Jean Glass, 2022).

2. **Discovering New Languages:** Learning a new language is more than just grasping vocabulary and grammar (Lori Jean Glass, 2022). It offers a portal into diverse cultures and mindsets, fostering open-mindedness and enhancing cognitive flexibility. Every word learned is a step towards a broader worldview.

3. **The Joy of New Hobbies**: Delving into a fresh hobby ignites passion and curiosity. Whether painting, dancing, or any other pursuit, it provides an escape from routine, stimulates the brain, and offers a fresh perspective on life's simple joys.

4. **Keep your personal space warm**: Reinventing your space to make it warmer and inviting enhances well-being. From adding cozy throws to infusing calming scents, these adjustments act as daily reminders of self-care and the importance of mental peace.

5. **Facing your fear**: Confronting and understanding one's fears is empowering. Recognizing what holds you back provides the clarity to address it, converting barriers into stepping stones toward self-confidence and courage.

6. **The Dawn's Early Light:** Waking up early offers a tranquil start, presenting a fresh canvas daily (Lori Jean Glass, 2022). This quietness can be utilized for introspection, planning, or simply soaking in

the calm. Early risers often report heightened productivity and a more positive mindset.

7. **Physical Vitality as a Keystone:** Physical fitness isn't just about aesthetics; it's a testament to discipline and self-care. Regular exercise releases endorphins, the body's feel-good chemicals, leading to a sharper mind, improved mood, and heightened self-esteem. Your body is your most extended commitment; cherishing it leads to holistic growth.

8. **Letters Across Time:** Penning a letter to your future self is a profound act of self-awareness. It crystallizes your current aspirations, fears, and learnings. When you revisit it in the future, you'll see the strides you've made, providing clarity and motivation to continue evolving.

9. **The Power of Constructive Feedback:** While self-reflection is crucial, external perspectives can be enlightening. Actively seek honest feedback. Others' insights can illuminate blind spots and offer new avenues for improvement, aiding in charting a more informed personal growth path.

10. **Embrace and Reflect:** Recognize your strengths and vulnerabilities. Embrace them, for they make you uniquely you (Lori Jean Glass, 2022). Set aside moments for deep reflection, asking yourself challenging questions. This practice helps you understand your core values, desires, and areas awaiting growth.

11. **Habitual Healing**: Our daily habits, often taken for granted, form the very foundation of our lives. By identifying patterns that don't serve us and methodically replacing them with ones that promote well-being, we craft a life aligned with our best selves. It's not about overhauling everything overnight but about consistent, mindful tweaks that, over time, compound into profound change.

12. **Step Out and Challenge Yourself:** Personal growth thrives outside the comfort zone. When you push yourself to try something new, tackle a challenging project, or face a long-standing fear, you're not just learning a skill or overcoming an obstacle. You're teaching yourself resilience, adaptability, and the invaluable lesson that you're capable of more than you imagined.

13. **Rest and Reset**: While action propels growth, pauses amplify it. Intentional rest periods, whether through meditation, short sabbaticals, or digital detoxes, allow us to assimilate our learnings, refresh our spirits, and bounce back with heightened vigor (Lori Jean Glass, 2022). Remember, we often find our most profound insights in moments of tranquility.

14. **Guided Growth through Coaching:** Sometimes, the path to personal growth can feel labyrinthine. In such times, a coach acts as a beacon. Their expertise provides structure to your growth

204 | S.G. FONTES

journey, offers fresh perspectives, challenges your limiting beliefs, and holds you accountable. Their external vantage point often illuminates internal terrains you may have missed.

While challenging yourself to move out of your comfort zone is not an easy task, it is undoubtedly a worthwhile one. So, my dear reader, take the chance and challenge your limiting beliefs. Remember, the only barrier between you and success is the self-limiting belief you have imposed on yourself.

THE SILVER LINING OF LONG-DISTANCE LOVE: HOW BEING APART CAN ACTUALLY BENEFIT YOUR PERSONAL GROWTH

When it comes to personal growth, one may expect that growing with a partner can only be possible if they are physically present. Well, what if I told you those miles between you two are not just spaces. Instead, those are opportunities for personal growth. Confused? Well, let me explain how:

- **Boosted Self-Awareness**: The solitude of long-distance relationships gives you time to dive deep into your thoughts, helping you better understand yourself and your desires. When we are with someone else, our decisions are often influenced by what they want/like. A long-distance relationship allows you to make decisions without chains bounding you to responsibility.

- **Communication Masterclass**: Distance compels you to get innovative in communication. Believe it or not, honing your skills to convey feelings and concerns more effectively.
- **Rediscovering You**: Being apart gives you the unique opportunity to delve into interests or passions you might've put on hold. Ever wanted to learn the guitar? Now's your time!
- **Resilience Builder**: Weathering the LDR storm strengthens your emotional resilience, preparing you for any challenges love throws your way.

Remember, every sunrise you witness alone is a step closer to personal growth and the day you reunite stronger than ever! So, always have faith in what is to come.

TIPS FOR SELF-IMPROVEMENT IN RELATIONSHIPS

Nurturing yourself and your relationship simultaneously can be a beautiful dance. Let's take a look at some twirls and steps to guide you:

- **Open Ears, Open Heart**: Listen actively to your partner. It's not just about hearing words but understanding the emotions and intentions behind them.

- **Solo Time:** Sounds counterintuitive, but spending time alone helps you recharge. A clearer mind and soul can contribute better to the relationship.
- **Growth Together**: Attend workshops or read books together. Shared learning brings shared change.
- **Set Personal Boundaries**: Know your limits and communicate them. It's a sign of self-respect and sets the foundation for mutual respect.
- **Celebrate Small Wins**: Each step towards personal growth is a victory. Celebrate it together or individually. It fuels motivation and joy.

Keep shining, and remember, love is a growth journey for both of you! Focusing on these self-improvement tips can help you evade the cloud of overthinking in the long run.

WHY A GROWTH MINDSET IS KEY TO ACHIEVING A FULFILLING AND SUCCESSFUL RELATIONSHIP

Relationships are beautiful, intricate dances of emotions, trust, and understanding. However, the lens through which we view them often originates from past experiences, lessons from our upbringing, and societal expectations.

Mindset in Relationship

Apart from loving one another, relationships also involve continuously growing with them. Two mindsets dictate how one approaches relationships: the fixed and growth mindsets.

Fixed vs. Growth Mindset

With a fixed mindset, individuals believe that their traits are static. They think, "This is just the way I am," which can make change seem impossible. Contrastingly, those with a growth mindset understand that traits and abilities can be developed through dedication and effort. They're more open to embracing challenges, learning from failures, and evolving with experiences.

Fixed Mindset Examples:

In a fixed mindset, your thought pattern may look something like this;

- Overthinking is just who I am.
- No text back must mean my partner doesn't care.
- I need constant reassurance to feel secure.
- Their actions prove they don't love me if they differ from my expectations.
- Overthinking indicates a problem in our relationship.
- Past hurts dictate my suspicious nature.
- I must control everything to avoid pain.

- Trust issues lead me to second-guess my partner.
- Worrying ensures I won't ruin the relationship.

Growing Mindset Examples:

The upside is that you can change the fixed mindset to a growing one. That may look something like this;

- Working on mindfulness to counteract overthinking.
- Giving my partner space, understanding they have their own lives.
- Building intrinsic trust in the relationship.
- Being open to different perspectives and needs.
- Believing that with self-awareness, overthinking can be managed.
- Healing and moving beyond past traumas.
- Choosing trust over control.
- Embracing vulnerability for a stronger bond.
- Using self-care techniques to manage anxiety.

Mind Reading

Another crucial part of a fixed mindset that will land your relationship into murky waters is when you expect your partner to read your mind. Misunderstandings arise when we assume our partners should instinctively know what we think and feel. Instead of discussing and clarifying, this mindset might think: "No text back must mean they don't care." Instead, work on turning your thoughts into proactive ones, like being open to your partner about your perspectives and needs.

Agreeing on Everything

It's a myth that couples should always be on the same page. Having different perspectives is healthy. It's how these differences are approached that defines relationship success.

Problems indicate Character Flaws

A fixed mindset may interpret relationship challenges as inherent flaws in one's character. For instance, "Their different actions prove they don't love me," or "Overthinking indicates a problem in our relationship." The truth is that everyone has a different upbringing and a different outlook on life. A simple conversation carried face to face may ease these confusions in your relationship.

Remember, embracing a growth mindset in love means continuously striving for better understanding, communication, and trust. It's about evolving together, ensuring the relationship remains alive, passionate, and resilient. Relationships aren't about perfection but growth, effort, and understanding.

Moreover, self-improvement is a continuous journey, vital both individually and in relationships. It enhances communication, trust, and emotional understanding. By understanding oneself, empathy towards others increases.

In relationships, it's crucial to balance personal growth with the relationship's needs, with both partners supporting each other's development and shared objectives. In the next chapter, I will walk you through the best ways you and your partner can plan for the future.

10

PLANNING FOR THE FUTURE

Relationships are like nurturing a plant. With the right amount of water, sunlight, and care, you can help a plant bloom. Similarly, in relationships, love and intention to care can help you both to thrive together. This chapter will delve into the art of nurturing your relationship for lasting contentment and joy.

Every stage offers unique joys and challenges in a relationship, from the initial spark to the golden years. But how do you ensure the flame never flickers out?

HERE ARE MY TOP 10 SIMPLE WAYS TO HAVE A
FULFILLING RELATIONSHIP

1. Live without expectations

Avoid setting up your relationship for failure with unrealistic expectations. Embrace surprises and adapt to changes. You'll find joy in unexpected places by letting the relationship flow naturally.

2. Focus on improving your flaws

Self-awareness is key. Recognize and work on your imperfections. When both partners engage in self-improvement, the relationship becomes a place of mutual growth.

3. Be calm before the storm

Every relationship faces challenges. Practicing patience and calmness during good times will help you navigate the rough patches more smoothly.

4. Set boundaries

A fulfilling relationship respects individuality. Set boundaries to maintain your personal space and ensure mutual respect.

5. Develop your sense of direction

While partnerships are about 'us,' it's essential to remember the 'me.' Have personal goals and ambitions to maintain your identity within the relationship.

6. Be curious about your partner

There's always something new to discover. Ask questions, show interest, and appreciate the ever-evolving nature of your partner.

7. Step away from the crowd

While societal opinions matter, prioritize what's best for your relationship. Personal decisions should be based on mutual agreement rather than external pressure.

8. Develop a common purpose

Find shared goals or passions. Whether traveling, charity work, or a shared hobby, these everyday pursuits can strengthen your bond.

9. Be hungry for personal development

Personal growth benefits the individual and the relationship. Engage in activities that enhance your skills, knowledge, and well-being, and encourage your partner to do the same.

10. Surround yourself with positive people

The company you keep influences your relationship. Engage with those who uplift you, offer wisdom, and inspire positivity in your love life.

Remember, every relationship is unique. These factors can always be tailored to fit what's best for you and your partner.

STRATEGIES FOR SETTING GOALS AND PLANNING FOR THE FUTURE WITH YOUR PARTNER

Navigating a relationship is like embarking on a thrilling journey. As you go, wouldn't it be fantastic to have a roadmap? Setting relationship goals with your partner is akin to sketching out that roadmap.

How to Get Clear on Your Love Goals

The first step is clarity. Instead of vague desires, aim for sharp, clear visions. Want to travel together? Specify where. Are you desiring better communication? Determine what that looks like for both of you. Clarity is the compass guiding your relationship journey.

What Are Relationship Goals?

These are shared objectives you both commit to. They could be anything from cultivating mutual understanding, planning regular date nights, or saving for a shared future goal. You both align with the 'We want this, and we're in it together' mantra.

How to Set Goals: A Normal and Healthy Part of a Relationship

Setting goals isn't about stringent rules but growth and shared aspirations. Here's a strategy that you can follow:

- **Choose a neutral space to discuss relationship goals**: This ensures both partners feel safe and relaxed. Your favorite cafe or a quiet park?
- **Determine the length of time for each relationship goal**: Some goals might be short-term, like planning a weekend getaway, while others could span years, such as buying a home.
- **Set check-in dates for each relationship goal**: Regularly discuss your progress. These check-ins are like pit stops, ensuring you're on track.
- **Include at least one fun relationship goal**: Remember, it's not all work. It could be learning to cook a dish together or taking dance lessons.
- **Ensure your relationship goals are measurable**: "Spending more time together" is vague, but "two date nights a month" is quantifiable.

- **Evaluate how your love goals make you feel**: Goals should excite and inspire, not cause dread.
- **Make sure your couple's goals are equally weighted**: Balance is essential. Both partners should feel their aspirations are recognized and valued.

Yes, it requires dedication and time to set these markers. But, as Nina Atwood wisely pointed out, couples who actively engage together tend to thrive longer. The journey becomes more joyful and purposeful, and the route more scenic when you have clear markers along the way.

Relationship Couples Goals Sample:

1. Define your love goals as a couple:

- What do you want to achieve in your relationship? (Examples: better communication, more quality time, greater intimacy, etc.)
- Why are these goals important to you as a couple?
- How will achieving these goals improve your relationship?

2. Establish a plan for achieving your goals:

- What specific actions will you take to accomplish each goal?
- How often will you work on these actions?

- What obstacles might you encounter, and how will you overcome them?
- What resources or support do you need to accomplish your goals?

3. Track your progress:

- How will you know if you're making progress toward your goals?
- What milestones can you set to track your progress?
- How will you celebrate when you reach each milestone?

4. Evaluate and adjust your goals as needed:

- What feedback have you received from each other?
- How can you use this feedback to refine or adjust your goals?
- What new goals can you set for your relationship once you achieve your current ones?

Remember to constantly review your goals periodically. This simple act will help you establish a great bond in the long run.

HOW TO STAY COMMITTED TO YOUR RELATIONSHIP

Commitment, at its core, is a conscious choice to stay devoted and steadfast to one person. It's much more than just a title or wearing a ring. It means being there for your partner through thick and thin, the highs and the lows. Commitment implies a level of maturity, respect, and a mutual understanding that you're both in this journey together, navigating life's challenges hand in hand.

Why is commitment important in a relationship? Commitment serves as the foundational bedrock of a healthy relationship. It fosters trust, ensuring both partners feel secure and valued. This security provides a conducive environment for love to flourish, promotes emotional intimacy, and offers stability, even during stormy phases.

With commitment, couples are better equipped to face and resolve conflicts, knowing that giving up isn't the first option.

Tips on how to stay committed in a relationship:

Let's look at some tips to stay committed in a relationship.

1. Regularly check in with each other. Voice concerns, share joys, and ensure you're both on the same page.

2. Whether it's a vacation plan, a financial milestone, or a lifestyle choice, shared objectives can pull you together.

3. Carving out moments exclusively for each other in today's bustling world is essential. It could be a simple date night or a walk in the park.

4. Instead of always aiming for agreement, strive to understand your partner's perspective. This act will build empathy and deepen trust.

5. Remember the little things that made you both fall in love. Surprise notes, random acts of kindness, or an unexpected hug can reignite the passion.

6. Acknowledge your mistakes and strive to be better. Being committed means constantly evolving for the sake of the relationship.

In the end, commitment in a relationship is about creating a harmonious space where both individuals grow, love freely, and face life's intricacies unitedly. It's an ongoing journey that requires effort, understanding, and, most importantly, an unwavering decision to stay together.

So, always remember, dear reader, commitment in relationships is the conscious decision to stand by one's partner through life's ups and downs. It's foundational for a relationship's health, creating trust and emotional safety.

This bond allows love to bloom and offers resilience during conflicts. To nurture commitment, couples should maintain open communication, set mutual goals, priori-

tize quality moments together, and cultivate understanding.

Occasional romantic gestures can keep the passion alive.
Additionally, acknowledging errors and striving for
growth is pivotal. Ultimately, commitment is about
forging a nurturing space where both partners flourish,
facing life's challenges as a united front. It's about
constant growth and unwavering togetherness.

Spread the Message of Love!

We're all looking for love… and we all need a little help to find our feet within it. This is your chance to help another reader find theirs!

Simply by sharing your honest opinion of this book and a little about your own journey, you'll show your fellow relationship overthinkers where they can find the help they're looking for.

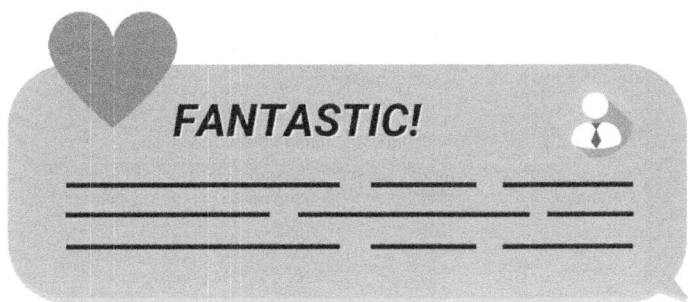

Thank you so much for your support. I wish you a future filled with love and happiness.

CONCLUSION

Like all good things in life, my friend, our journey has ended too. Throughout these pages, dear reader, I hope to have offered you a treasure trove of insights into managing the sometimes tricky waters of intimate relationships. By mastering the methods I talked about, I hope you can navigate your relationship with a newfound sense of confidence and assurance. Remember, it's not merely about keeping the boat afloat; it's about setting its course toward more vibrant horizons.

Importantly, before we part ways, I want you to remember the mantra of healthy communication and self-care. Let's face it—expressing our innermost feelings, desires, and boundaries can sometimes feel like a Herculean task. However, by learning the art of transparent and empathetic communication, you can foster a deeper bond marked by mutual respect and understanding. When couples share, listen, and support each other's self-care routines, the foundation of their relationship grows stronger, ensuring they can weather any storm.

I understand that reflecting on our past can be a double-edged sword; memories can bring smiles, yet there is also some pain. Despite these challenges, exploring these recesses of our minds is crucial. When you courageously confront your past experiences and patterns, they glean invaluable insights into your behaviors and thought processes. Such self-awareness can pave the way for transformational personal growth as individuals and in the dynamic you share with your partner.

Now that the path has been illuminated, it's time to embark on this transformative journey. Dive deep, learn, grow, and cherish the love you and your partner build together. Remember, every relationship has its challenges, but with the right tools and mindset, the journey can be incredibly rewarding.

The process, though demanding at times, pays off by weaving a tighter bond between partners. I hope to have provided you with ways to set, monitor, and celebrate milestones in your relationship. From defining love goals to tracking progress and making necessary adjustments, the relationship evolves into a deeply rooted bond.

Dear cherished reader, armed with a treasure trove of wisdom, profound insights, and practical strategies, you now possess the keys to nurture a profound and heartwarming connection with your beloved. Together, you'll embark on a journey of personal and shared growth, bound by a love that deepens with every passing day.

The time has come for you to take these invaluable tools and set out to paint the canvas of your relationship with vibrant colors of joy and understanding. Like a skilled artist, you're poised to craft a masterpiece of love, one that evolves and thrives with each stroke of care and commitment.

If this book has illuminated your path and added warmth to your understanding of the beauty in relationships, we invite you to share your thoughts on Amazon. Your heartfelt feedback isn't just a review; it's a ripple in the pond, a gesture of kindness that helps spread the message of love, growth, and togetherness to others who seek to find the same profound connection you've discovered.

With immense gratitude for being part of this journey, we extend our heartfelt wishes for your love story to continue flourishing and inspiring those around you. Embrace this journey of love and growth, and let its radiance touch not only your heart but the hearts of countless others.

REFERENCES

Brickel, R. E., MA, & LMFT. (2017, September 15). *How to Build Trust in a Healing Relationship as a Trauma Survivor*. Brickel and Associates LLC. https://brickelandassociates.com/healing-relationship-trust-after-trauma/

Capanna-Hodge, D. R. (2021, December 12). *15 Tips to Practice Gratitude For Better Mental Health*. Dr. Roseann. https://drroseann.com/15-tips-to-practice-gratitude-for-better-mental-health/

Cindy. (2023, February 12). *How to Build Healthy Relationships After Trauma*. CindyTalks. https://www.cindytalks.com/how-to-build-healthy-relationships-after-trauma/

Davin, K. (2022, September 12). *Impacts of Lack of Communication in a Relationship & 13 Ways to Improve*. Choosing Therapy. https://www.choosingtherapy.com/lack-of-communication-in-a-relationship/

Dr Josh. (2018, July 17). *Natural Remedies for Anxiety: 15 Ways to Relax Find Calm - Dr. Axe*. Dr. Axe. https://draxe.com/health/natural-remedies-anxiety/

Earnshaw, E. (2014, June 12). *How Lack Of Communication Sneakily Ruins Relationships*. Mindbodygreen. https://www.mindbodygreen.com/articles/lack-of-communication-in-relationships

Edberg, Henrik. "34 Quotes to Help You to Stop Overthinking (+ My 5 Favorite Tips)." The Positivity Blog. Last modified June 1, 2023. https://www.positivityblog.com/overthinking-quotes/

Gepp, K. (2022, August 29). *How to Let Go of Past Hurts: 8 Ways to Move On*. Psych Central. https://psychcentral.com/blog/how-to-let-go-of-the-past-and-hurt

Glass, L. J. (2019, January 22). *Why Is Trust Important in a Relationship | Relationship Workshop*. PIVOT. https://www.lovetopivot.com/the-importance-of-trust-in-a-relationship/

Gupta, S. (2021, December 27). *How to Build Trust in a Relationship*. Verywell Mind. https://www.verywellmind.com/how-to-build-trust-in-a-relationship-5207611

Kubala, J. (2019, March 20). *Magnesium for Anxiety: How You Can Fight Anxiety and Feel Better.* Healthline. https://www.healthline.com/health/magnesium-anxiety

Lebow, H. (2016, May 17). *Become a Better Listener: Active Listening.* Psych Central. https://psychcentral.com/lib/become-a-better-listener-active-listening

Lehal, M. (2018, March 29). *5 Ways to Show Your Partner You Care -- Just by Being Mindful.* Psych Central. https://psychcentral.com/blog/5-ways-to-show-your-partner-you-care-just-by-being-mindful#1

LMFT, R. E. B., M. A. (2017, September 6). *How to Find Healing in Relationships After Trauma.* PsychAlive. https://www.psychalive.org/find-healing-relationships-trauma/

Marshall, C. (2020, July 30). *What To Do if You Don't Trust Your Partner.* Self Space. https://theselfspace.com/what-to-do-if-you-dont-trust-your-partner/

MasterClass. (2022, May 13). *How to Stop Overthinking in a Relationship: 4 Tips.* https://www.masterclass.com/articles/how-to-stop-overthinking-in-a-relationship

McDermott, A. (2021, December 15). *Natural Remedies for Anxiety: 10 Ideas.* Healthline. https://www.healthline.com/health/natural-ways-to-reduce-anxiety

McDermott, N., & Spann, R. (2022, November 9). *How Gratitude Can Transform Your Mental Health.* Forbes Health. https://www.forbes.com/health/mind/mental-health-benefits-of-gratitude/

Mental Health America. (2022). *What is GABA?* Mental Health America. https://mhanational.org/what-gaba

Mind. (2021, February). *Anxiety signs and symptoms.* Www.mind.org.uk. https://www.mind.org.uk/information-support/types-of-mental-health-problems/anxiety-and-panic-attacks/symptoms/

Mindful Staff. (2020, July 8). *What is mindfulness?* Mindful. https://www.mindful.org/what-is-mindfulness/

Mueller, J. (2018, July 5). *Love Languages.* Growthtrac Ministries. https://www.marriagetrac.com/love-languages/?gclid=Cj0KCQjw2qKmBhCfARIsAFy8buLPDjWum6uXXEjO1iPx_j0tAUcvJT6Pr2wE0pPRG-wkMIN-HX71wAcaAqvhEALw_wcB

Nguyen, J. (2021, August 18). *This Is What You Need To Do To Actually Get*

Over Someone — Once & For All. Mindbodygreen. https://www.mind
bodygreen.com/articles/how-to-get-over-someone

Omega 3 Innovations. (2018, December 3). *How Omega-3 Fish Oil Can
Benefit Anxiety Disorders*. Omega3 Innovations. https://omega3innova
tions.com/blog/omega-3s-for-anxiety-unpacking-the-benefits/

Phil, D. (2022). *Relationship Communication Test | Dr. Phil*. Www.drphil.-
com. https://www.drphil.com/pages/rct/

Polk, J. (2022, February 23). *What Causes Insecurity in a Relationship? How
to Stop Feeling Insecure*. WikiHow. https://www.wikihow.com/What-
Causes-Insecurity-in-a-Relationship

Psychology Today. (2019). *Gratitude | Psychology Today*. Psychology
Today. https://www.psychologytoday.com/us/basics/gratitude

Raypole, C. (2019, August 9). *How to Rebuild Trust After a Betrayal*. Healthline; Healthline Media. https://www.healthline.com/health/how-to-
rebuild-trust

Regan, S. (2020, December 22). *Meet Your "Shadow Self": What It Is, When
It Forms & How To Work With It*. Mindbodygreen. https://www.mind
bodygreen.com/articles/what-is-shadow-work

Self Care Impact. (2021, February 5). *Is a Past Trauma Impacting Your
Current Relationship? How to Tell - Lakewood & Longmont CO*. Self-
careimpact.com.   https://selfcareimpact.com/is-a-past-trauma-
impacting-your-current-relationship-how-to-tell/

Sheppard, S. (2021, September 12). *Jealousy: Characteristics, Causes, and
Coping Mechanisms*. Verywell Mind. https://www.verywellmind.com/
what-is-jealousy-5190471

Shepperd, S. (2022, June 8). *Can Vitamin B Improve Your Mental Health?*
Verywell Mind. https://www.verywellmind.com/the-mental-health-
benefits-of-vitamin-b-complex-5322841

Smith, S. (2019, July 23). *How to Handle Overthinking in a Relationship*.
Marriage Advice - Expert Marriage Tips & Advice. https://www.
marriage.com/advice/relationship/is-overthinking-in-a-relation
ship-bad-for-you/

Therapist Aid. (2018). *Grounding Techniques*. https://www.therapistaid.
com/worksheets/grounding-techniques

Trieu, T. (2020, December 31). *5 Signs You May Need To Heal Your Inner
Child & How To Start*. Mindbodygreen. https://www.mindbodygreen.

com/articles/inner-child-work

Unilacke, K. (2018, February 6). *17 Warning Signs That Overthinking Is Wrecking Your Relationship*. A Conscious Rethink. https://www.acon sciousrethink.com/7206/signs-overthinking-wrecking-relationship/

Weber, J. P. (2018). *When Past Romantic Trauma Damages Your Current Relationship | Psychology Today*. Www.psychologytoday.com. https://www.psychologytoday.com/us/blog/having-sex-wanting-intimacy/201802/when-past-romantic-trauma-damages-your-current-rela tionship

Will Meek. (2019). *How Anxiety May Affect Relationships: Are You Dependent or Avoidant?* Verywell Mind. https://www.verywellmind.com/how-anxiety-can-cause-relationship-problems-1393090

Writer, J. L., News. (2022, June 13). *"Overcome Your Overthinking" Shows Benefits of Gratitude Practice*. Wondrium Daily. https://www.wondri umdaily.com/overcome-your-overthinking-shows-benefits-of-grati tude-practice/

Made in the USA
Las Vegas, NV
13 May 2024

89875100R10128